JOYFUL DAYS AHEAD

GIOVANNI MARCO CALZONE
JOYFUL DAYS AHEAD

with contributions by Luigi Giussani
and Giacomo Tantardini

JOYFUL DAYS AHEAD

By Giovanni Marco Calzone

Original Title: Si prospettano giorni felici

Translated from Italian by: Fr. Matthew Henry

Edited by: Suzanne Tanzi

Copyright © 2012 Marietti Publishing House S.p.A
Genova-Milano

Copyright © 2025 Human Adventure Books
17105 Longacres Ln
Odessa, FL 33556

www.humanadventurebooks.com

All rights reserved

ISBN: 978-1-941457-34-4

Contents

Foreword | 1

For a Friend | 3

Biographical Introduction | 5

From nature springs fear of death. From grace, audacity. | 7

Joyful Days Ahead | 11

Easter Spiritual Exercises of the University Students of Communion and Liberation | 128

Assembly of the Community of Communion and Liberation in Campania with Luigi Giussani | 146

Funeral Homily | 159

Joyful Days Ahead
…. because I asked the Lord to be able to serve Him

Foreword

Giovanni was a very reflective person. He had the habit of writing down his thoughts on pages of loose-leaf paper or on old notebooks, which he also used for Philosophy classes or School of Community meetings. Since the day of his death, we have held in our hands a boundless world that, being a shy and reserved person, Giovanni expressed freely in this way.

Some of his notes were collected by Father Giacomo Tantardini for the funeral homily, and they soon ended up in the hands of Father Giussani, who offered them to the university students of Communion and Liberation (CLU) during the Spiritual Exercises that took place around a month after the death of Giovanni and his friend Massimo.

In 1990, a short work was published containing a large part of the material collected in this book, which had the title that we also propose now: *Joyful Days Ahead*, the beginning of a thought that Giovanni concluded with "…because I have asked the Lord to be able to serve Him."

Father Giussani often expressed the desire to publish this little booklet. And so the experience of Giovanni is now offered to everyone, together with the comments of Father Giussani given 30 days after his death, as well as at the Easter Exercises of the CLU (March 1988) and at the summer gathering of CLU leaders, the Équipe, in August 1992.

The Calzone Family

For a Friend

As I read again the contributions in this little volume that those who love the life of Giovanni have carefully collected, the recollection of those moments that are by now chronologically distant come crowding in on me. They are very alive in an experience that Giovanni offers us still today. It was well into February 1988 when, just recently married, I was travelling often between Avellino and Naples to continue, together with a small but lively group of university students, the great adventure of loving knowledge that Father Giussani had opened up in our lives. This handful of people, over the course of two years, had already recognized the discreet presence of Giovanni who, above all with his silence, but sometimes with his energetic dedication to each gesture and each proposal of the companionship, *felt* himself growing in personal awareness. He was moving at a fast pace, compared to the rest of us, to become the absolute protagonist of his own adventure of faith.

Father Giussani warned, in *Traces of the Christian Experience*, that we need to guard against easy enthusiasm. For those who engage in the great adventure of Christian life, it quickly becomes clear that the point of the struggle is to become adults in every aspect of existence, in a way as fascinating as it is demanding.

Giovanni quickly grasped the necessity of comparing all the aspects of existence with the light of the Christian proposal, which he encountered in the movement of Communion and Liberation, and in the long and frequent visits to my house, where he continually asked what I thought of this or that aspect of his choices and decisions. He did not want to give in to the mentality of the world, but rather to train himself to judge everything in light of the discovery of Christ in his life. We would discover how true this training was only at the end when, facing the brilliant prospects of the future, while life opened up to him with promises of joy and full satisfaction, he wrote, "Joyful days are coming because I have asked the Lord to be able to serve Him."

What strikes me the most, remembering Giovanni's story, is his maturity in front of everything and his openness in sharing every part of his daily life. Giovanni had decided in his great heart that nothing and no one could fulfill him except the Lord, who had educated him to love and follow that fragile sign that is the Christian companionship. He had understood the deepest consequences of this companionship, and those depths have been in time the doors of grace that his sacrifice opened for the story of our community in Naples. In time, the awareness of many of us grew, in a way unthinkable at that time, of the generosity needed in facing the sacrifices that belonging to Him asked of us. There grew a story that Jesus began through the poverty of our faces marked deeply by the cry still present in our hearts: *Joyful days are coming because we ask the Lord to be able to follow Him.*

There remains today, in this great human experience, the living presence of Father Luigi Giussani's voice, a voice that accompanies us every day through the loving presence of the Christian friendship that asks us again, as it asked Giovanni then: *But you, do you love Me more than everything?*

Tonino Romano

Biographical Introduction

Giovanni Marco Calzone, born in 1962, was the third of six children from a family of solid Catholic faith. After a happy childhood, his adolescence was characterized by an ever more urgent search for the meaning of life. For this reason, after graduating from classical high school in Benevento, he enrolled in Philosophy at the University of Naples.

A long and troubled period of searching for an answer to his desire for happiness resulted first in his active participation in a youth political movement, then in the establishment of a cultural center together with some friends.

In 1982, Father Ilario Gallucci, his confessor, told him that his sensibility and radicality were close to those of Communion and Liberation (CL). Giovanni asked to meet some people from CL and began to spend time with them, first in Benevento and then in Naples. He participated in the Spiritual Exercises for university students in 1983 in Fiuggi. Everything began from there.

A friend invited him to move to Naples to live the university experience more intensely, and he agreed without hesitation. The encounter with CL had an explosive effect on his life, as well as the lives of his friends and family. This encounter enriched every part of his life. He continued to do the same things as before: he studied, he dedicated hours to attentively listening to music, he went to the pub with friends. But now everything he did was pregnant with reason, with purpose, and with joy.

After graduating with a degree in Philosophy, he taught in two Neapolitan classical high schools. He resumed the activities of the cultural center he had been involved with, with a new determination generated by the desire to communicate the beauty he had encountered. A few days before his death, he confided to his sister: "You know, I have the impression that every gesture of mine springs directly from faith and I am aware of it. It is like there is no longer anything between me and God."

On the morning of February 21, 1988, Giovanni was on the road to Campitello Matese, a ski resort where he was accompanying some students. A head-on collision, caused by the sudden onset of illness of the driver of the other car, caused the death of Giovanni, of his friend Massimo Cioncada, and of the wife of the driver of the other car.

From nature springs fear of death. From grace, audacity.[1]

Luigi Giussani

Life is *for*, whatever may be the content of this *for*: life is a tension, a motion, a *movement*. But this movement is described by the alternatives in the following phrase: *From nature springs fear of death. From grace, audacity* (this is not from a modern existentialist, but rather from Saint Thomas Aquinas, and comes to us from the height of the Middle Ages). From nature, which our mother gives us, emerges the fear of death; that is, from nature that is in motion, there arises a *counter-action* that strangles our energy. From grace, instead, there emerges not *happiness*, but audacity, that is, a dramatic definition of life, life as a path and a struggle. But what is this grace that overcomes the first part of the phrase (*the fear of death*) and offers another version of life (*audacity*)? Let us pause on this word audacity.

Audacity, in the first place, implies *the affirmation of a purpose*. Otherwise it would not be audacity, but stupidity. If someone flies along in his car at 110 miles per hour, three yards from a cliff, it would not be audacity but stupidity. Audacity implies an intelligent recognition, the awareness of a purpose.

---

1. From *Dalla natura, il terrore della morte. Dall grazia, l'audacia*. CLU Équipe—La Thuile, August 1991 in *Il Sabato*, n. 4 (1992), pp. 47–53, then in Luigi Giussani, *Un avvenimento di vita, cioé una storia*, Edit-Il Sabato, Milan-Rome (1993), pp. 307–317.

"At the end of the day, Jesus said to His disciples: 'Let us cross over to the other shore'" (*Matthew* 14:22). Here, this crossing over—from the shore where the disciples seemed to be planted—to the other shore, this crossing is, *in action*, audacity: it affirms something true. It affirms, that is, that the truth of their existence was not the edge of the lake where Christ had fed the people, but something else, the other shore.

There is a connection between the farther shore and the shore where Christ had fed the people: the farther shore was the purpose for which he had fed them. While they all were still holding on to the miracle that had just happened, Christ said to His followers, "Let us cross over to the other shore." Which means: the truth, the meaning of that which we have done and we are doing, the origin, the consistency and the destiny of the miracle that happened is something else, not the bread, not the fish, not the infatuation of the crowd.

Audacity, therefore, implies the *awareness of a purpose*, of a destiny, that is *something other* (Mystery, Other) than what we know, what we touch, what we do. But that awareness is not enough. Audacity implies also an energetic impulse, an impulse that sustains the path, an energy that makes one press on through the waters and the fog in the journey toward the Mystery, toward the other shore.

Emblematic of this audacity is *La Navigazione* by Andrea Pisano (a little sculpture that we used as the image for the Easter Poster this year). There are two disciples there in the boat, rowing, moving through the waters of the sea toward the other shore, both of them intent and yet, at the same time, calm and secure. Jesus is behind them in the boat. The journey, the passage, the crossing toward destiny, becomes possible only when there is *a presence* (if one were rowing alone, he wouldn't be able to navigate, he would cease moving). The path becomes simple if there is a presence–that is, to be clear, if there is *a companionship*. *From grace, there surges audacity* comes to mean: from a Presence other than us, audacity

From nature springs fear of death. From grace, audacity.

wells up in us. Grace is a Presence from which audacity springs (like one who comes up behind us and pushes us forward).

If existence is movement, we must *decide* for this movement, that is, decide for existence. But if our very nature, which is movement, produces a counter-movement that suffocates our energy, while grace gives us audacity, *to decide for existence* means *to follow* the Presence that makes audacity surge up in us, that makes life a continual movement. Only if man takes the risk of deciding (as those two disciples in the boat did), can he travel toward the other shore, which means that he truly adheres to reality, making life the journey to reality. Otherwise, he sinks, because "from nature comes the fear of death." (Certainly, there is a simple way to avoid all this: *to cut off* the head or *tear out* the heart.)

There is a corollary in what we have said that I want to emphasize. If the two navigators sculpted by Pisano had rowed by *calculating*, that is, for example, by saying, *Within three, thirty, or three hundred yards we should reach the shore, the shore should be there, we will be able to discover reality*, they would have been foolish. *What do you know about destiny?* It is right to say, "I would like to see God," as one of our songs says, "but it is not possible."

Our dear friend Giovanni understood this well (his death is one of the greatest sacrifices that God has asked of us). In the first paragraph of this book, which is a collection of his thoughts, he affirms, "Good will and an open heart are not enough anymore. We cannot delude ourselves into thinking we can give everything. In fact, everything is given according to a measure that is proper to the whole. We need an openness to the immediate, setting-in-motion of the self. [This is like the two disciples in the boat, who are at every instant open to the setting-in-motion of the self, indefinitely—there is no preestablished end in their movement. From grace there surges forth an audacity that makes one open to the immediate setting-in-motion of the self.] We never reach this "everything." But the point is not to reach this everything, but to search for signs constantly. We need an openness that goes beyond what is required by religious precepts or formulas. We have to set out on an adventure in which you are not the one who calculates."

This is life, and whoever does not accept this does not accept life: "You have to set out on an adventure in which you are not the one who calculates." But is there something that can make us embrace life more and more, that makes us more united as we pursue the unknown, which audacity penetrates with the strength of a presence? There is an intensity of affection that is born precisely from the inability to calculate, revealing that we are in the hands of an Other.

Joyful Days Ahead

Giovanni Marco Calzone

Good will is not enough

Good will and an open heart are not enough anymore. We cannot trick ourselves into giving everything. In fact, we must give everything according to a measure that is proper to the whole, to the big picture. We need an openness to the immediate setting-in-motion of the self. We never arrive at this everything. But the point is not to arrive at this everything, but constantly to search for signs. We need an openness that goes beyond what is required by religious precepts or formulas. We have to set out on an adventure in which you are not the one who calculates.

Anxiety

The reason why we are anxious is this: we incorrectly believe that the reality about which we are anxious is essential for our life. That, and at the same time we do not acknowledge a Reality whose horizon is much bigger—the Beauty which men no longer believe exists.

Anxiety as a symptom of idolatry

Anxiety is the fear of losing a good. But the Good cannot be lost, because it is faithful. Anxiety reveals our attachment to partial goods that condition or determine our life. When there is no anxiety, there is instead the certainty of not being able to lose the whole.

Even though we can sometimes fool ourselves into believing that we need something now that is objectively illusory, still, we cannot fool ourselves about our desire for life, a desire that is disturbed by the thought of death. Here it becomes clear that only God can resolve this problem.

Living is never banal if we remember that the Infinite is mysterious and powerful and destroys all our idols, even those that are most persuasive. There is always, in every instant, even if it does not seem to be the case, the possibility of transcending the sphere of the obvious and continuing on the second journey. Everything exhausts itself. The Infinite does not. To open ourselves means to stand with an open mind, listening for that which all things hide. How much we are immersed in the mist of the obvious and of idols!!!

If the possibility of familiarizing ourselves with the meaning of everything does not exist, how can we live? The strong man is the one who, after any adversity, returning to himself, recognizes a meaning that envelops that event. If I, after anything happens to me, returning to myself, do not have the capacity to say truly, *I belong*, and in this pronouncement to find my peace, or at least to glimpse it, I am still immature. The possibility of maturity is linked to the existence of the sign and the instrument that carries with it an objective Meaning.

Pain for the Christian

The Christian is marked out among other people by having a complete vision of reality, a vision that does not exclude anything, not even pain. Even pain, within the horizon of Christian meaning, is taken up and given value. It may seem that in front of a perspective that has a positive outcome (hope), pain should disappear. In front of the fact that the one who holds all things is our closest Friend, it would seem that pain should not have any rational foundation. But, despite all this, pain exists and conditions; it determines life. There is a disproportion between reality, which is maximally positive and ultimately triumphant, and the soul that suffers. The satisfying truth, recognized with reason, does not change the emotional condition through which we have to walk. The reality we encounter that introduces us into another dimension does not have the strength, at least insofar as we can understand it, to overcome sadness. It is like saying that our capacity to respond is weaker than our emotions. (But what is the root of this affection? Does it have a positive cause? It seems like it does not.) The truth we encountered should involve mind and heart, or else it could not determine the state of soul that results, the decisive opening of all the human components (reason, emotion, etc.), It is a mysterious force that makes us live, that keeps us tied to things; it is an energy that lifts us. In the measure in which it is in us, we live with positivity, openness, and passion. Confidence is the fruit of this energy. Pain is when this energy is lacking. It is a force that exists, but could be missing, and in fact does disappear sometimes; therefore, it is a gift. Pain makes us understand that the energy that makes us is a gift. We have to make two decisions when sadness rules and everything drifts apart, losing its traits, its outlines, its face, to the point of no longer saying anything. The first is to beg for life to return to us. We must reawaken the memory of the Event we have encountered, reconnecting to the abundant source of life. The second decision is to accept the situation in which we find ourselves, giving it a meaning and considering it necessary so that something even greater can happen in our life. But all this does not have value if the Light, if God, does not accompany us. Pain is given so that we can pray more and better.

The problem is to find something on which we can fix our attention in order to overcome our difficulties. I need to focus on these areas: study, perfectionism, introversion, pensiveness, scrupulosity, vigilance, gossip. For each of these things I need to pay particular attention. Understand, though, that if my mind is fixed on some area, it is not focused on others. Is there a center on which I can place my attention, concentrate my energy, so as to avoid being dispersed in a multitude of areas, and which, at the same time, allows me to walk a path that encompasses everything, without leaving anything out? I need, at this point, to expand upon that Christian hypothesis: "Seek first the Kingdom and His righteousness and all these things will be given to you besides" (*Matthew* 6:33).

The search for truth

Seeking the Kingdom means seeking in every moment the truth of things, of attitudes. The alternative to this path is letting ourselves be determined by our natural attitude, by the opinion of the *world*. The natural way of triviality presents itself to us immediately; it is the wide path that invites us to measure things according to the prejudices of the time and not according to the perennial value of the Truth. Above and below that *wide path*, there is the path of Truth. Triviality, banality, is that level where we continuously live. Near this level we glimpse the dimension of authenticity. *Seeking the Kingdom* means looking for the stable value of study, of work, of our other actions. In the measure that human activities are open to the infinite, they are morally positive. The authentic attitude is reawakened either by pain or by age; better still if it is reawakened daily by reflecting on what we are doing. "[A]ll these things will be given to you besides" (*Matthew* 6:33) means that, in overcoming the *ordinary* and living in the *exceptional*, we let go of what passion makes us desire in the moment, and find everything again after having faced the (apparent) risk. And so, studying only because we have an exam is surpassed by studying while keeping before us the whole of life.

If one asks, "What counts more for you: your passion (whatever it may be) or your faith?" and you respond that your passion counts more, then you are a pagan. If you say that your faith counts more and you devalue that passion (which in itself is positive) and renounce it, you are being moralistic. If instead, you join that passion to the Ideal, and only in view of the Ideal does that passion have meaning for you, then you are a Christian.

Measure

It is that natural part of man, the part that requires a continual education, which is shaped above all by the structural law of reality.

The measure of things

Nervous conditions, phobias, and scruples demonstrate that reason is not the measure of everything. There is, beyond reason, a meaning of things within which reason exists and should be immersed like a sponge in water.

The true man does not let himself be defined by circumstances, because it is he that defines circumstances through a judgment.

Symbols

We need symbols (i.e. signs, sacraments), because these respond to the desire for something definite and, at the same time, to the desire for infinite openness. Symbols strike us emotionally and seize us with their sensible force. They lead us to something beyond. They define but they do not exhaust, or, better, they evoke by nurturing an undefined passion that starts from a familiar object. Symbols open up dimensions and help us avoid turning the infinite into a poetic or existential confusion.

Memory and law

There is only one thing that makes us grow, that should be defended before all else: memory. Memory introduces us to the level of authenticity, the heart, where we perceive deeply our fundamental and decisive needs. Memory is the awareness of a powerful question and of a solid and definitive answer. Defense of memory is, in an Augustinian way of thinking, defense of the unity that does not change. In our dispersed thoughts, our words thrown out without judgment, in our abundance of empty words, in the actions that make us forget and do not allow for the re-composition of the various factors, because there is no consistent beginning—in all this, multiplicity triumphs and weakens man. Precepts either defend memory or else they are rules that lack life and require a voluntaristic application that moves out of habit. The problem is not one of respecting laws but of living life and making use of every instrument and every indication.

In fact, when one enters into authenticity, he breaks onto a new level. It is a new dimension of thought and another *actuality*.

Beyond intelligence and will

The most honest rigorism is not enough, nor is clarity of principles. The strongest will is not enough, nor the most intense care for the world. The most Christian philosophy is not sufficient, nor the most Catholic doctrine. Until it goes beyond the sphere of intelligence and the sphere of will, Christianity is not actualized. The point is truth in the present, that is, correspondence in the present between that which is and that which we have encountered. Only when this correspondence in the present is at a fundamental, authentic level, can we speak of **memory**.

The full decision, beyond the substantial immutability of the horizon of life

When we think only of a partial goal, which, once reached, we say that we will return to living, this is the idolatry that brings us to the threshold of the level where faith plays out. The passing years present motives that claim to impose themselves on life: graduation, job, marriage, etc. We need, in the present, within these circumstances, something that transfigures them. A renewed Christianity launches us into a drama between its content and the human measure. Christianity does not tell us to disregard the things said earlier, but to seek for them without presumption; both Christianity and the common mentality compete to realize a particular project. Within the concern for these things a drama is born; to live the drama means to take advantage of the *critical period*, which is a particular occasion to take a step forward. Tomorrow will be like today. New worries hound us without touching the most interesting part in us. Either we live within these worries or we come to the point of involving the whole person in a full decision.

Realism and memory

Realism, understood as the overcoming of the mechanism by which we project a scheme on things, the ideologies and thoughts let loose by reality, is what leads, technically, to *compunctio cordis* (re-awakening the heart), to memory understood as the reconquering of the unity of the person in the present moment.

Something positive, something ultimate

It is not enough for us to have a peaceful soul and to preserve a distance in front of things and an impassability in front of pain. We want our heart to be in turmoil, to beat with suffering if nothing else. Nor is the desperation of an agitated, disturbed heart enough. It is not enough to be proud of the anguish of which we are aware. We now want to see something positive that makes us live vigorously. Prayer should produce a certainty; otherwise, it is only a vain lament on the sad fate that has happened to us. It is only a highly poetic gesture. We are hungry for certainty, not for desperation.

Humility

Humility is the recognition of a measure different from our own, a true measure. It is not passivity. The recognition of a greater measure certainly involves a renunciation, but it does not entail passivity. Humility is accompanied by the perception of a Positive that is accepted, that gives strength.

Legitimate nihilism

The current problem is treating intermediate values with a lack of respect. There is only one absolute value, one end: the **search**. Intermediate values are instruments, but they become instruments that are so important (in some cases and some circumstances) that they seem essential. Starting from the certainty that the means for the search have been given to us and will always be given to us, why then do we get blocked in front of intermediate values? A relationship with a woman sometimes seems like the only instrument. In fact, that is how she is perceived. Passion weakens us, because energy, naturally meant to be directed toward the search for God, instead is dispersed. The true human face is marked by a profound freedom; it has nothing to lose–not women, not power. We need a kind of Nietzschean irreverence in order to destroy idolatry. We fall into idolatry when we search elsewhere, not in the true place; when we confuse the intermediate value with the absolute value. It is not here that you should look. Our goal is somewhere else. We must set out together. Our aim is unique. We need to destroy the intermediate thoughts when these insinuate themselves without permission, illegitimately. We need to clear out space, *Nietzsche-like*.

Knock and it will be opened to you, seek and you will find

("New possibilities for knowing ourselves")[2]

Man is called to search; the search consists in going beyond the appearance of things to catch their essence. In everything there is a depth that does not appear immediately but that can be reached. The end of man is to know, a knowledge connected to blessedness. The search is sustained by the fascination of the new, by *opening wide* to the world of life. There is a fog that reduces and annihilates vision. The promise consists in this, in the possibility of venturing into new horizons. *Finding* indicates the possibility of success for the one who decides to follow *knowledge*. Finding is an existential opening. Only this saves a relationship. We must join, in any case, the *world of life*, beyond logic, beyond the pre-established scheme of words.

---

2. Battiato, Franco. "La stagione dell'amore" ["The Season of Love"], in *Orizzonti perduti [Lost Horizons]*, 1983.

Re-opening the human problem

The point is to pronounce the decisive **You** to the only stable Reality. To choose among different idols (the idol is a good unfastened from absolute reality) the **You** that dwells in a horizon within which it is possible to find serenity beyond the appearance that comes into being, arises, and dies. To live life as belonging is to bind your mind to the **You**, because then your thoughts are centered and stable. The crisis of the secular world is the crisis of the supremacy of changeability, becoming, over Being. To be familiar with the horizon of Being is to believe that there is a reality that does not appear which is more stable, more true. This Reality, this **You**, is the origin of every thought and every action. But the way of reactivity is more immediate. Falling in love is often not born from this belonging, but from a mushy sentimentalism. The problem here is the point of departure. In this kind of romance, you have to cut out the **You**, the origin and end of everything that happens in life. But there is a tiny comma separating the autonomy of a particular from mental stability, from familiarity with that **You**. You can't think of anything else.

The horizon of the sacred

Our pain stems from the fact that we have come to live outside of the horizon of the sacred. Our everyday horizon changes with the change of circumstances. But the horizon that is defined by the circumstances is suffocating; attractive at the beginning, it then becomes boring. Living within this type of horizon, we adjust and try to put the pieces of ourselves in order. But the numbers never add up. By horizon, we mean that which immediately comes to your mind.

In many cases, the fear of the outcome (in relationship with others, for example) conditions us and we do not dare to risk. We always start from the presupposition that we should succeed, that we should create a positive reaction. When we glimpse the possibility of a practical failure, we get discouraged and give up.

We are the servants of an invisible master (i.e., a cancer), that does not show its face but only confuses us. And this confusion is our slavery. The confusion is in not having a knowledgeable center that takes on everything, not having a principle of action from which to start.

To give a meaning to pain means to bring all of our own pain to the *quintessential*. Existentially, every moment is instructive. Every feeling has a meaning insofar as it has already been felt by the one who is the explanation of the human enigma.

To live a wide open horizon is to do everything according to a positive will (a free *yes*, a submission), without being subject to the situation, without being determined. Even when we *follow*, we need the positive will to follow.

Pain that is accepted is the Christian paradox. Uncertainty: in front of the circumstances. (Uncertainty is present when the circumstances dominate.) For the Christian, certainty is found in being above the law.

In theory, we can dream of following an intermediate position, something that is in the middle. In practical reality, this dream vanishes. Man, in the moment he acts, makes an absolute choice (often implicit), not an intermediate one.

And what if the Lord wills that your image in the sight of others be a difficult and distorted image? The point is not to be well-loved and esteemed, but to be free from our own image.

The law is at the service of a new dimension, not an end in itself.

The sense of belonging as a stable horizon
Memory can be lived constantly as the condition that envelops every moment of life. It is a vigilance that does not end, a closeness of affection that we perceive, of which we are aware. It is the heart that, awakened, accompanies every thought and every action. The work to do lies in facing the intense moments of the day out of a familiarity with the newness we have encountered; this newness, at

least once, has struck us, has corresponded to us. Our only hope is that it may become more and more familiar. This is like when we are studying, and we need to repeat something over and over until we know it by heart. Later, this exercise becomes less heavy, even though it must become continuous—in the same way it happens in the field of the heart. Belonging as a stable horizon, in the sense of the effects that it produces in the soul, is comparable to a state of excitement, but one that endures.

Desire for a gaze

The deepest perspective is from the heart, even though it is often overclouded or censored. The heart is rarely touched; even more rarely is its most intimate part captured. To be seized at the root of our very "I" does not depend on the will, on sacrifices, on openness–it is a grace. There is a difference between an emotion and the strong presence of something decisive for life. There is an innate and constitutional desire to be loved, to be seen, in man. This desire (which then, consciously, becomes a question) already contains the beginning of its satisfaction. The encounter with friends and family who look you in the eye with expectation is first of all a reality. There exists an unknown reality behind the signs, a powerful reality, that does not pass away.

Natural and supernatural: the "revival"

The continuity between the natural and the supernatural is proven, for example, by the *intuition of death*, by the involuntary *reliving* of negative situations. A trauma that has happened in determinate circumstances is lived again, years later, when analogous circumstances present themselves; it is suffered anew. Analogically, there happens a *renewal* or a religious re-actualization, in a positive sense.

Being or nothingness

We must overcome the multiplicity of thoughts and reprimands, the turmoil that suffocates the voice. Beyond the tumult of the unconscious, there appears the radical alternative, existentially perceived, between being and nothingness (the emptiness of everything, the privation of partial satisfactions, of those that fill us, of beauties created by the mind, which we need to live). When we reach this threshold, we reach the point of the question.

Question and freedom

What is interesting is a free choice, the actualization now of a freedom without borders. There are hardened schemes in the world, and these schemes penetrate the mind. There are projects in the mind of man that can oppress other men. There are others that we treat like good projects, even Christian projects. What interests the perception of true freedom is beyond the consolidated schemes that the world proposes, is beyond the oppressive project, is beyond even the good project with a Christian slant. When we join our perception to the importance of a Christian choice, this is a step in the right direction; when we imagine our own life spent for the Christian project, that is something true in us. But we have not yet touched the point. Within Christianity, we tend, existentially, to reformulate a scheme over and over. Prayer then becomes the breaking of a reassuring scheme. It is putting ourselves in front of another. Prayer must lead through another way. This way, though, is painful and liberating. "For even as love crowns you so shall he crucify you. Even as he is for your growth so is he for your pruning. Even as he ascends to your height and caresses your tenderest branches that quiver in the sun, so shall he descend to your roots and shake them in their clinging to the earth."[3] Liberation is given by loving only that which can be loved without grief, only that which does not flee away.

Nihilism

All solemnity is lost; the authoritative voice no longer dares to speak; everything is low, debatable, mediocre. It is the end of enthusiasm toward Being. There is not an enthusiasm that raises us up, nor a deep joy, nor a strong passion. Everything is silent.

---

3. Gibran, Khalil. *The Prophet.* https://poets.org/poem/love-8.

There is no presence, no beauty; everything is tenuous now. Not even pain is too strong anymore; it is more like numbness. There remains only the pain of a lack, a lack that we notice, rarely, of a deep Beauty. Within this (sometimes) painful punishment, within the tiredness and the death of the heart, there yet remains a patient expectation of waking up.

Beyond need: the necessity of a strength

How unto just entreaties shall be deaf
Those substances, which, to give me desire
Of praying them, with one accord grew silent?

'Tis well that without end he should lament,
Who for the love of thing that doth not last
Eternally despoils him of that love![4]

When we perceive a love for ourselves, the sign of a gaze that always accompanies us and that cannot die if we do not want it to, we must accept it deeply and seek familiarity with it. The gaze of the Companionship is a sign; the sign requires us to go beyond; the sign must be actualized through meditation. The strength of life is given by the awareness of a constant gaze. We can follow this work profitably. It is the only content of a prayer that is certainly heard.

Introduction to the totality of reality: there is no maturity if there is not a point of reference that develops our person. Attracted by this Center, we desire to be like it. Normally, we are attracted by the particulars that touch our instincts. Affection is not a state of soul. Then (this is affection) it is natural to remain there; that spark that you have experienced is very practical. It is natural to be attracted and through this attraction the encounter becomes operative, practical. But in this relationship, the fundamental thing is to recognize that everything has been given. There exists in history one unique hypothesis of gratuitous relationship, without calculation, for you.

---

4. Dante, *Paradiso*, XV, vv. 7–12.

Offering and the I

One cannot offer unless he starts from a free gaze on himself (or at least, from a desire for this). This free gaze looks upon his own fundamental disposition. If he does not offer the fundamental disposition of himself, he does not offer himself, but the image that he has of himself. But what do I offer in an analysis motivated by my images? What do I write?

Do I offer the fundamental disposition of myself or the vagueness of my images that make me lose myself? Can one ever offer something if he forgets himself? But what do I offer if I am totally lost in the things that I have done or in the counterfeit image that I have of myself (that is, an image that does not respond to what I ultimately am)? I cannot offer anything. I offer my falseness. I offer myself. But I, when I say *I offer myself*," what am I saying? Which *self* am I talking about?

An offering cannot come from a prison; the offering must be free, but my *self* is in chains, because we are chained when we want to defend our own image. It is a good that you can lose and therefore it cannot be loved without worry. The *self* is forgotten when I repeat from memory phrases that I have heard in the Movement, when I speak the language of the Movement and never my own, when I make use of a ready-made discourse. What needs to come into play is everything, every aspect of my life. Everything should be considered. Everything should be faced. We must accept ourselves for what we are, looking at ourselves with simplicity. Among us it is not like this: we censor our weaknesses, our shyness, our fears, our difficulties, our misery, in the name of an image of ourselves that we have built with our own hands. We avoid drama and end up in aridity. We try to preserve, at best, the artificial image of ourselves, in front of ourselves and in front of others.

Instead of entrusting ourselves exclusively to what we can build out of this image, we are called to confront our own face with all the restlessness, the uncertainty, the weakness, and the anguish that characterizes us. The only real salvation that has been promised to man historically, telling him that all of his humanity must lead to this goal, whatever wickedness and whatever weakness, the only reality that has introduced in history the possibility of transforming everything that is in man, is Christianity. Within ideologies and in all human companionships, you must censor yourself in order to belong. You get nowhere by being as you are. Since I have been here, I have been going continually forward. The extraordinary thing is the speed with which things have gone. I should thank some people (when you are looked at in the face, you are better and you acquire new energy). The Movement is a fact linked to everyday life. The new impulse, which I had in the period before the vacation, has been at work even after; many things have changed in virtue of this new energy.

A natural fear emerges when I am away and when I have to do things foreign to me. The fear diminishes in the measure I draw near to the content of belonging. Without a foundation, you cannot build.

Fears? Accept them, because there is something more important that, after suffering, deep down, explains the suffering, giving it a complete response, and encompasses it. Desire: always less of a banner, more and more connected to the only credible support of my weakness. Often this awareness becomes a fallback on myself, creating problems for myself and not facing reality. It is no longer possible not to start from Christ. How can this personal awareness be at the origin of a new openness to reality? It does not have to do with managing to find a position. You must say who you are. Nor does it have to do with following a moralistic way. When I say "I," what do I express? (The fragility of the sense of belonging.) We must re-center our personal position around Christ. But most of the time, we belong to our thoughts and our projects.

The offering

This is the drama considered in its human realization. It is the practical side of the drama. The drama, in fact, is not to dream about a far-off ideal, invoking it poetically.

The question

To ask is to set up a human position in front of things in such a way that the content of the experience is newly represented (this is what we want to do). What credibility does a question have that does not engage one's own energy in a tension toward an answer? So, the attitude of the man who asks requires an openness to the effort and a "positivity" – a coming forward, a putting to good use.

Preamble

There is no offering, nor is there a question, if there is not, right out of the gate, a free gaze on yourself, on the fundamental structure of your own being. But what else does this fundamental structure of the self await but a true fulfillment?

The touched heart and the ghostly fog

No friendship, no set of roles touches the heart. The heart must be touched by something that satisfies it. Everything can touch the heart but everything can distance us from the heart. We touch the heart when we have a gaze that is free of ghosts. The ghosts are the forced maintenance of esteem, of friendship, of a role. This face, though, is not yours.

The Fragmented Person: The person that identifies the realization of self with the realization of a particular or of a series of particulars. There are those who succeed in doing this (except when there is a complication, because then the crisis comes in).

Stability: What sustains the offering and the question is the *person*. The fundamental structure of the *person* is the *person* considered in his essential needs, what remains once the cloud of dreams that determine the day are taken away.

The Offering is the concrete way of living the drama as a tension toward growth.

The Challenge is the putting to good use our own nature. It is a decision in the present. We do not need the past nor the future.

Ascesis: change

1) *Change does not happen through moralism.* The point of departure is a different gaze, an attention to yourself, a different companionship. It is not to live with gritted teeth.

2) *To get up again continually*, there must be something that is bigger than our own misery, or else we are stuck in ourselves, counting our falls or censoring them proudly, in order not to chip away at our own images.

3) *But towards what is it stretched?* If the point of departure is a free gaze on yourself (that you are not finished), the goal is the realization of this desire in its depths. Hope is the expectation of an outcome; our days are sad because we do not live in the certainty of the outcome.

Gratitude is to live in the awareness that the content of the Companionship is greater than your misery.

Pain always breaks the crust that hides the heart. But we are together so that the heart may always emerge.

Even the person formed by belonging is not worth more than the roof tile that can fall on top of him. He has value insofar as he is in the hands of an Other who holds him.

The point in question is the **nexus** (**breath**, **memory**, **present** – it is the instant that has value; the rest does not count, you do not count in reality) with the content of the Christian experience.

Everything is for the sake of returning to the heart. Everything is to be said starting from the heart.

We can escape from human effort thanks to a clear, free question. The freedom of the question means the freedom of the exercise of the intelligence and the will that has become mechanical and tiresome. The clarity in the question means a question starting from what we are deep down, beyond the thoughts that oppress you. They oppress you so much that you do not even know it is possible to discover that your authentic face is given even before the question of a man beaten in life who neither knows the reason nor has the strength to live.

Anxiety is overcome in a conscious offering of our time: to live as one *dependent upon*, as one *in function of*…

To escape from the usual turmoil of the ordinary horizon is possible only if a new dimension shows itself. To escape the usual turmoil is difficult. It implies the renunciation of our own ideology, which can be kept in check, but which blocks us from tasting life. The usual schemes have a fascination that soon disappears, that lasts only a short time. The personal project very quickly loses its attraction. We need to go beyond the traditional limits. We have the possibility of absolute freedom, the freedom of a naked man, just as he is in front of life and destiny. This is the freedom from obstacles, both from ourselves and from others, and is something fascinating: the possibility of spontaneity, the overcoming of a position that settles. To live the religious sense. To think only of the Kingdom.

Prayer is to hold up something different from the schemes that obscure the fundamental question and the content that responds to it. Actually, prayer is not to make my own instinctive aims prevail, but to attach myself to the truth, waiting for the path to be indicated to me.

Prayer is above the circumstances, the pains, the joys. It has to do with a dimension that is always valuable, whatever happens, whatever state of soul predominates.

From the painful awareness of a strong need to the perception of a stable certainty: prayer has nourished the road of this passage (prayer without doubt).

Today I make the effort to give witness: I am; my face is this story. It becomes stable. Happiness comes from communicating and asking intensely for Christ in things, in real circumstances.

From the offering up of distress to its overcoming... This exercise leads to a gradual penetration into the realm of the non-controllable. This comparison, carried out systematically, starting from the self, in the end does not touch only the reason but also the character, the emotions. We sense a fascination only in front of something greater than the self. The finite wears itself out. Either it goes beyond, accepting a greater measure, or it becomes boredom. We must single out the elements of a judgment of our experience.

— The day is either inserted into the perspective of meaning that transforms life into a history,* or it is wasted. These are the two alternatives from which there is no escape.

* History is a complex of gestures linked together by a meaning. The concept of history is linked to that of *homo viator*, which recalls the necessity of a constant and laborious construction.

— The hostile circumstance and the complex character that we find in ourselves are no longer a mortification when *nothing happens by chance*.

— It is not obvious that we have encountered something that totally takes hold of life. Idolatry also grabs us in a total way, but its disproportion is evident.

— As we engage in our studies, we either give in to a logic of power or the logic that consists in loving the Fact we have encountered. It is according to the logic of power to study with the preoccupation of reaching graduation as quickly as possible, studying for high grades, and with the preoccupation of exalting yourself. But to engage in studies or in any other circumstance is for the sake of continuing to walk, often with difficulty, on the only practical way.

Disorientation

Disorientation is when something is outside the horizon of meaning.

Memory is to know that we exist and to live in the perspective of *being at home*.

But I, when I say *I*, what do I think of? Of the one who returns my face to me, the face I have lost, or not?

Every ordinary human experience should be lived with intensity, tending toward a total immersion in the instant, for only one reason: Christianity is the fulfillment of every expectation of existence; it is lived with zeal only if we do not avoid ordinary circumstances, which occupy, in the general order of reality, the lower steps of a realm whose highest point is the sacred. What reality ultimately contains is the meaning that man is searching for.

The criticism of most definitions of the person is strictly connected with the education that tends to reduce itself to instruction. There is nothing to be formed in the subject, nothing to provoke maturity. There is no reality within which to introduce someone. There is no meaning. A principle is established that offers no criterion for facing reality. Then a tolerance that translates into a total suspicion in facing the problem of truth prevails.

The outcome of this conception seems to be the dismemberment of the subject in the net of power. In fact, the subject is not educated to cultivate a personal position, and so he is totally vulnerable in front of external solicitations. The person who receives an education that is reduced to instruction is valued only for the utility that he provides to society. He becomes an instrument in the hands of power.

What is truly awesome is that through an event, a reality is created around it whose characteristics surpass the intention of individuals. We come here to encounter people, to spend time. Maybe, unfortunately, the truer motive for which we should come is still in the dark (that is, the encounter with a reality that is beyond us). Still, this companionship, which humanly is formed for so many banal reasons and by a small grain of faith, has characteristics of absolute gratuity, more or less hidden (it also depends on the way in which we see things). The community is interested in you without wanting anything in return. This companionship is, for you, a small or great possibility (it depends on the strength of the companionship) of change for the better. It is the experience of goodness, the encounter with an attitude that gives value to what you are, that gives hope to what you will be. The experience of goodness is ordinarily tied to an intersubjective relationship, to a companionship that may be different, that manages to get the best out of you, that indicates to you the steps, that puts you in front of immediate hopes.

We must choose between a life made of moments unconnected among themselves, without a logical thread, a casual adventure, without head or tail; a life lived in pursuit of the moment we must reach later, a life lived running toward a future that, when it becomes present, dissolves *without meaning* in your hands. The other solution is to choose to have a history, made up of various experiences that are united in a meaning. To have a history is possible in a companionship, because the voyage, alone, is too difficult, impossible for us. To have a history means to look behind ourselves and to recognize that we have grown, that year after year we have become greater.

The one who sees has a great advantage over the one who does not see, which is that he can say that he has seen reality, that it is true. He can also say that the one who has not seen has his eyes closed. How can the one who has not seen respond to the one who has eyes to see and ears to hear? He does not know.

I no longer want to hear
Talk about fearful ghosts.
It has been hard, it is still hard
To escape from monstrous caves.
There was no family
There only remained the mark

Carried for a long time in the heart
A brand registered by fate:
Forever sick with alcohol.
But then there will be the encounter
With Him who forgives everything
With the One found in the midst of the others
Who guides us on the path and spurs us on
The encounter has been enough
The divine heat has returned.

The cloak of time distresses us
And we who aspire to another
Raise our hands and sing
To Him who was dead and is alive.
You transcend the rock of time
You reopen the doors that will never shut.
Begin to hope again
Because its flow will not be in vain.

The dominion of self is a victory, not the absence of a battle. In order to attain this victory, as a man, one must ground himself in that which unites him and not in that which separates him from other men (reason).

The itinerary of faith

The expression should be understood in this way: what is proposed to us is the road that others before us have walked. The path has been marked out; it is up to us to follow it or not.

    We are invited to verify a hypothesis of life. We thus understand how the religious fact is something greater than an ideology (a lot of human words) and that it is not reduced to a collection of precepts. Religiosity is thus a fact already lived by others that have found in this fact the Answer to their needs. The itinerary of faith that has already been outlined by other men is placed before us. We will know how to behave ourselves coherently if we do not reject the hypothesis before verifying it and if we are disposed to accept it after having verified it—to live what we have experienced, and nothing less.

The history of the Hebrew people is our history. Whoever has experienced His presence, even confusedly; whoever has experienced it as a source of change already has a road, has something that he must remember.

There is a depth of the self that cannot be denied; it is hidden, but all that is needed is an insult, a trifle, a word to bring it to light. When this deep-down pride is touched, there arises a suffering and the possibility to react, seeking the lost ground, seeking to recreate in the mind the image of ourselves that we have. But, next to this, there is another possibility: that of a *dispossession* of self at the level that has been touched.

The trace of this depth is something in the heart that we reach after having learned this position (of dispossession) in front of things. There is a trace to follow that remains always and everywhere; it does not depend on the circumstances, which can even become an occasion to follow this trace. This trace is beyond efficiency, success, fascination, capacity. The only necessary element is the person.

The true perspective—or, if you will, the Way, understood as the trace, as a dimension of the heart—is the way through which life again enters the person whose woundedness makes him judge himself unfortunate or incapable of knowing and living reality. The perspective that we are talking about gives equal dignity to the one who is not fully functioning.

The fear of disturbing others by telling them what we have encountered means that we are not certain that what we are proposing is truly ours, truly capable of changing lives. The error is twofold: we think that this event is *our own thing* while instead it is a proposal for everyone; or else we are uncertain about the fact that this event is more powerful than we think and that it does not depend on us.

Energy

The source of energy comes from the act of faith. The act of faith is an act of dispossession wherein we entrust ourselves to an Other, we renounce our idols. Or, in favorable circumstances, the source of energy is gratitude, which means that the realities we have are not ours, nor are they owed to us, but they have been given to us and can be taken from us as well. In ordinary circumstances, the act of faith is in the true approach to the question, even if we do not feel it emotionally. The act of faith is an event that brings man to the fountain of his being. This fountain is not in the relationship with a woman, but in the relationship with the community. For this reason, there does not exist a basis of *continuity* of the relationship of two, as if the subject is supported by the other, finds his energy in the other. The relationship is founded on a personal decision, the act of faith.

Openness and presentiment

1. By openness, we understand the dimension of the soul that faces the contingencies of life by referring to an origin without limits, the only one adequate for man.

2. Openness is the dimension that contradicts whatever absolutizes a particular, because the particular has a short breath. After a little while, it falls into boredom and slavery. Anyway, absolutizing a particular contradicts the deepest need of the heart.

3. Presentiment, understood as love, is, in the field of morality, the only thing that respects the infinite impulse of man, that which opens and does not close itself in front of the particulars of life.

4. Presentiment is not necessarily the *moment* before action, understood in a chronological sense; it is above all the first **motive** of action. In the measure in which we return to the origin, that is, we make *the act of faith*, the dimension of the heart is respected and developed.

Loss of the tension

What a difference between a dialogue stretched toward discovering another, perceiving always in front of itself a mystery that is interesting to discover, that, recovered, leads to the other; and a chat that just passes the time, in expectation that something comes about in the future, something that maybe is already planned out! What an abyssal difference between a random gathering of people, a permanence that is merely formal, and that initial period of falling in love.

This tension is gradually lost and we tolerate this loss without reaction. Our day is made up of moments that are more or less interesting, but there is no plot.

Boredom

When the present is without content and the future looks heavy, because there is no stimulus that fosters action, this is the time of boredom. Boredom is that feeling that we experience when things do not speak. When this feeling becomes familiar to man, we begin to speak about nihilism. Nihilism is the philosophical position characterized by belief in nothing, when things don't say anything. Boredom, as a ghostly silence in which nothing is heard, is the negation of the symbolic mentality. It is the abyss of inauthenticity; it is the ordinary that becomes so normal that it does not encounter anything else. It is the triumph of the *old*. The *new* instead is the leap of the soul in front of a reality that speaks to and engages us. It is the renewal of the invitation, the prospect of new possibilities, of new projects, of new horizons.

The emergence of reason

We have the feeling, after some action or some discussion, that some plan should come out of it, reducing what is provoked by the circumstances, what is nourished by events independent of us. The person who decides, the person who is free, the person who reasons more and who is always less immersed in the indistinct level of half-sleep should emerge in the clearest way.

Close and hidden beauty

Surrounded everywhere by beauty that awaits being discovered and enjoyed, we, day after day, instant after instant, lose occasions, putting off the necessary effort to an indeterminate *tomorrow*, without understanding the absoluteness of the present moment.

But things still wait to be uncovered. (By *uncovered*, here I mean that human act that consists in overcoming *obviousness*, putting ourselves in an *authentic* position.)

Moralism

It is the setting of a life that must decide the outcome of a particular behavior in a particular circumstance, not vice versa. This is to say that, in practice, the general aspect counts more than the moralistic one.

Detachment or instinct—passion or nihilism

Detachment: "I said in my heart, 'Come, now, let me put you to the test of pleasure and the enjoyment of good things.' See, this too was vanity. Of laughter I said: 'Mad!' and of mirth: 'What good does this do?'" (*Ecclesiastes* 2:2).

Instinct: Instinct is the attachment to a good that is held to be decisive for one's own destiny and is not our destiny.

— This good that we love is not infinite and thus is not enough for a desire that is without limits.

— This good is not attained and thus generates vain fatigue, and certainly anxiety.

— This good is not preserved: it can end; its attraction soon wears out.

Passion: The effect of an authentic cultural position: created things as expression of hidden richness; sensible reality as an instrument, as an openness, as the revelation of *new possibilities*. "From one single Word, everything…" (*Imitation of Christ*, Book I, 3, 8).

Nihilism: An unthinkable distance from things, bringing boredom. Reality is supported by nothing, does not say anything.

Detachment threatens the domination of partial values, the ironic gaze on bourgeois worries (the *good things*), as the function of an absolute affirmation. This detachment is a *making space* [reception] that will not become nihilism [emptiness, denial]. Passion is the attachment to the multiplicity of reality that is the sign of an initial Unity. If the transcendence of the sign does not happen, it gets trapped in a disordered and infantile passion.

The law of the real

The desire to prevail, to overcome our own environment, to save a situation without respect to its limits, means not submitting ourselves to this law. Reality, thus lived, sooner or later rebels. Careful attention with the desire to force others to respond positively produces an emptiness. We go beyond the limit when anxiety comes in. Anxiety is provoked by the will to reach what we cannot determine, what is not part of our sphere. With respect to falling in love, it is the same. Reality reveals it. There is no need to construct it ourselves. Reality is contemplated, not forced. In front of reality, we stand and listen, paying attention to the signs.

There is no piety that can stand up against the evidence of the real.

Judgment

The link between elementary experience and reality is given by judgment. Reality, understood globally, including the current horizon, made of atheism and chaos, is something negative in itself; "Everything conspires to silence us,"[5] nothing fosters the emergence of the person. Men lose themselves in contact with reality. But there are exceptions: we know that, despite what has been described, we have grown humanly. The point is a criterion from which to begin to express a judgment; the negativity of a situation

---

5. "Everything conspires to silence us, partly with shame, partly with unspeakable hope." Rainer Maria Rilke, *Duino Elegies*, Elegy II, vv. 42–44.

is overcome by judgment, because judgment makes a man free from everything. Judgment is the recognition of an actual reality: Christ has won; with judgment we participate in this victory. Judgment is the connection of the individual with the Meaning of everything, it is to recognize and participate in a reality of facts; it is the affirmation of faith. And faith, when it exists, conquers the world. Judgment is to face things starting from the person in his fundamental structure, that is, from Christ, who is the answer to our human question.

The Christian method today and the Cultural Center

A Cultural Center today can only assume a secondary position. In the contemporary world, in which the word has been devalued by too much use, it is more than ever evident that salvation comes from the encounter with a Fact, not from the encounter with the cultural consequences of that Fact. We should not fall into the presumption that we are able to skip steps. In the Middle Ages, culture exploded after centuries of lived Christianity. We skip steps when we fill the room by forcing people to be there. If we arrive at the point of needing to fill up a room by force, we have lost the way. Culture should arise out of a natural fact. There are few people who remain curious (I do not say more) because of a coherent and exhaustive cultural conception. Today we need to start living again. Conferences may be outdated as a method, but if we are not to skip steps, to defeat the power of the current culture is a duty. Today, the commitment to culture is above all—and not for everyone—a personal duty we need to develop.

The fundamental dimension

It is certainly not our work that changes things; change is caused by the grace that intervenes when we ask for it. The fundamental dimension of existence is the question. It is difficult to understand this truth from the relationship between two people, where it seems like everything depends on us. Nothing could be more false. The *openness* of the heart of the other does not depend on force, nor on control, nor on an education. In these cases, as in all the others, we must assume an attitude of entreaty, that in practice is translated into following the truth in daily circumstances. If this is the fundamental dimension at the existential level, ontologically we can begin to speak about the metaphysics of the problem.

The lack of openness to give our religious testimony in a language that is understandable to everyone, to propose Christianity in terms that are *less unacceptable* for a soul far from the faith, but rather to give a nude and crude religious affirmation—all this is pride. It's a desire to serve the self and not the truth. The attitude of service leads to making ourselves weak with the weak, strong with the strong. This lack of elasticity is a sign that we want to present only what we have in our own head.

We are not dealing with the voluntaristic effort to see things as if they were beautiful and good when they really aren't; we are dealing only with recognizing Reality as it is, contemplating it without prejudices, without sentimentalisms linked to the moment. We need to stretch ourselves continually to remember the Positivity that we have discovered, which existed before us. Therefore, we have to contemplate it, not create it.

Western culture is distinguished from Eastern because it accepts reality as a useful instrument for ascesis. Ascesis, according to an Eastern and also Platonic perspective, consists in *overcoming* physical reality by penetrating to the authentic, which is metaphysics. Catholicity distinguishes itself in this: that reality in itself, in its richness, is the instrument used by Being to communicate itself. Adhesion to Being, on the part of the individual, comes through adhesion to the circumstances. Reality is a hidden richness to uncover. The soul is launched toward the external world starting from a horizon of meaning that embraces the root of the person. The Catholic is turned outward, because everything is meaningful, and openness to reality is the way to realize the self.

Horizon

When Saint Paul says, "I consider everything as loss..." he is not referring to realities or circumstances, but to dimensions, to all the dimensions of the heart that are outside the Christian perspective. We can say dimension or horizon. Every man has his vision of things, has his heart turned toward an ideal. The gaze on this ideal generates a perspective of awareness and action that constitutes his *vision of the world*.

The manipulation of reality: mediation

The engagement with reality in truth, starting from an awareness of belonging that gives us strength to open ourselves, leads to a movement that begins from a position of meaning. In facing the circumstances, there are two factors at play: the person and reality. The approach to reality on the part of the person starts from a conception of things—in Christian terms, from a memory, that existentially is the motive for action. But Christianity does not demand a comfortable application of faith to life, but rather motivates us to use our intelligence and to direct the things that can be manipulated in a more authentic and just way. To speak of memory means to inform our own conscience that faith is the decisive factor of life, and on the basis of this faith, our conscience thinks and acts. The Christian person bends himself to reality after bending himself to Being in the acceptance of belonging. Reality is complex, and facing it requires the submission of the person to its laws. Every dimension has its rules: study, play, the organization of initiatives. We cannot have faith and not act: faith is that which gives meaning and therefore encourages and requires the total use of intelligence, which is called to submit itself to the inexorable laws of Being, that touch all the apparently banal rules of study that call for efficiency, of play that pushes us to victory, of initiatives that demand success. A discussion like this, outside of a religious vision, falls into mere efficiency. If, instead, it begins from faith, it outlines an important stage of maturity. The manipulation of reality should happen within memory and thus should begin from the heart, understood biblically.

There are adverse circumstances, apparently insignificant, but they conceal a particular meaning (like a stimulus to overcome a barrier; thus we keep our vigilance): the study of a particular material, the duty to face one's own edgy character, the noise that fills a large part of the day, etc.

In life, so far, almost all my dreams have come true. What is left of these realized dreams? Nothing. The problem is that after succeeding in something, this satisfaction, in the instant it is fulfilled, disappears. The most favorable circumstances, as well as the ugliest ones, are cancelled out by time. Is it possible for something to remain? A gaze on what you are: either it grows or it diminishes.

What interests us is what really happens.

In reality we try to break the cage of nihilism.

In reality we try to recover the religious sense.

In reality we try to recover a cyclical conception of time.

These and other things give witness to an actual change.

Saint Thomas made the distinction between the things we think and the things that exist. We should be interested in the things that exist, that already actually exist. A change in thought is not enough; we need a change in fact. It is not enough to study Eliade and say that the cyclical conception of time is right and just. We need to speak about it only after we live time in this way. The understanding of the above-mentioned phenomena is nourished by the historical framework, by the gaze on universal history that simplifies the relation.

Critical periods

Life presents *critical periods,* that is, spaces of time in which the surrounding factors push us to make a choice. In these critical periods, so named by analogy with psychological ones, if a leap is not made, some sort of growth in formation, it does not happen again. These periods put us cruelly in front of an alternative.

After an escape

Every day and many times in a day, we must make the decision to be open in front of the circumstances. Sometimes, the moments in which we must decide pass over us and we don't recognize them; we live without exercising a vigilance over ourselves. In these cases, most of the time, our instincts prevail, instincts which try to defend ourselves from the *extraneous* and close us in front of things. We defend ourselves thus, with our arm raised, protecting our secure, calm, horizon, a horizon that is comforting but narrow. We do not open ourselves to new things that can change us. But the day after the escape, we realize that we have lost an opportunity.

The question

"The one who seeks finds…" (*Luke* 11:10). We hope for a result. The question is proper to the man who is free of images, desires, partial and prearranged aims.[6] The free gaze on yourself. Hope is the origin of joy, since it inserts a horizon that has an opening; it makes us already glimpse its fulfillment. We must start from the situation through which we are passing; we are not trying to overcome the moment in time but to live it. We cannot say that our seriousness in front of things will begin tomorrow, because the present disposes you to the future and as you are today so you will be tomorrow. In our days, there is something like a drama; flatness and grayness seems to predominate. Things, instead of calling to us, are lost to us. Daily we become aware of the misery that is in us. A recognition of this type is the beginning of a request: that the fundamental intuition be present in our days. A day is saved when we recognize our own misery and loyally turn our gaze to our person in its constitutive need, in its expectation of redemption. But if we remain attracted by the persuasion of the content that the companionship brings, what remains to be done if not

---

6. We all have these, but we can't be defined or limited by them.

to propose again a familiarity with this content? A Christianity unlinked to the self/person is moralism, a series of duties; your self is not involved. Either we belong to the companionship or we belong to our own fluctuating and directionless heads, or to others in a less human way, unaware, or to the circumstances, in the sense that these set the tone. The outcome of the circumstances determines our life. We are at the mercy of this. What really gives meaning even to the adverse circumstances either does not appear or appears only with difficulty.

You open your eyes in front of the value of the relationship (which is a love for yourself, beyond your capacities and your efforts). You gain the result in time if you ask for it because in an instant you have seen the true image of yourself.

—The request is the expression of what you are.

—Christ is different from what you think.

The certainty of change comes because, for at least one moment, you have experienced a correspondence.

In front of the difficulty, either we count on our own strength or we go to the origin. In the first case, we rely on our pride, we are nourished by a pretense. In the second case, we live in the truth. Hope is a certainty in the future because of a present fact. (The reality that you have before you—you either face starting from yourself or starting from a present fact.) Or you have nothing.
Sheer willpower does not pay off, because the person is weak even when he seems strong. (Starting from the self, we come to want only the self.) Hope, that is, projecting yourself toward reality, facing what you have in front of you, requires a good reason, a foundation, because reality is scary, and you can accept the risk only when there is a good reason. Immaturity: we do not go to the heart of the question; memory requires that we pass through the heart.

The principle with which we face reality: if we do not open ourselves to things, we will just be chatting (we have to ask, this asking is our responsibility). To live with truth means that one remembers the truth as a thing that time makes always more beautiful. Why am I certain that this is not a waste of time? We all have two things in common: 1) My hope is founded on the heart. Each of us is born with a need for truth, a need to be welcomed. Then the years of life suffocate this heart, but they cannot destroy it. We can close in on ourselves—it is as if we no longer expect anything. Life tries to suffocate this perspective. This great horizon exists by nature, a positivity that is never deluded. There is a desire that does not empty you. The greatest evil is to close yourself to this expectation, to expect nothing. We can act as if we have already arrived. We must rather be open to a possible newness. Everything conspires to numb this expectation. But it cannot be totally destroyed. Some people have made me glimpse that there is an answer; we can find a response to this evident desire. 2) In life it is possible to encounter a good for which the heart waits. Something, at least for a moment, tugs at you. If the horizon is not infinite, it suffocates. It is possible to encounter this You in a human way.

Even in our studies, we cannot sever the link between efficiency (a realism to the point of the particular) and memory (which becomes existential in adhering to things). Study is useful when you have a motive for living. We do not take a decisive step in life, because we are overwhelmed by particular things in the world. We must be repeatedly deciding to live for Christ. Either we are Christians by name or we are Christians in order to risk.

We want Being to manifest itself to us and to others

Something must remain of the gestures we make. The beautiful or ugly impression passes. We are not talking about political advantage: in a few years everything could be totally different; all that we are concerned about will have passed. But something must remain. Otherwise, in the end, it will have been in vain; all this work for what? To keep our days busy? They are already busy. Personally, what remains has been an enlargement of horizons: to put my faith in play within an important initiative, to rely on something greater than my efforts. But above all there remains in me the discovery of a strong bond with my friends. Moreover, there remains the conception of the gesture as an event to serve. We are trying just to slip through life when we do not accept an order in the day, an effort. Our faith is still not strong enough to support and to accept an effort. Instead, it is only through an effort or a personal risk that life changes, in the sense of an unscrupulousness or, rather, a freedom from stress.

The conference went well. A week and more of preparation, work, embarrassment, people, anxiety, then success. What has remained of all this? Today is like the days before the conference. A philosophical change among us? What has changed after '85? How can we live reality in a way that something remains? In fact, something does remain: not the success, but the deeper friendship among us, a greater clarity about the dignity of the choice of faith, a humanity that has grown. What allows all this? What gives strength to face the work (which could be the conference, but also your studies, etc.) or the fear? What gives strength is only to live for a goal. How do we live for a goal? By asking for it. In the asking—if it is true—I affirm that the goal of my life is another. The worthiest, most human question is to ask the one who has conquered me to intervene in my life now.

Freedom of the heart means a distance from the values preached today, values like systematization. On the contrary, freedom of heart requires the personal courage to go forward in the day without expecting anything from the small projects. All time consumes, objectively and subjectively—subjectively, because what is important today becomes obvious tomorrow, loses the sense of newness that fascinates. Freedom is linked to a fullness of esteem. We must live for a goal that sooner or later is capable of awakening what we really need deep down. To live for a goal is a begging. We live for Christ because we have an urgent need for Him. The truth is that existentially, not intellectually, our thoughts are stronger than the living desire for our human growth; therefore, we cannot bear when another person talks about us. All the small goals imprison us. But there is a goal that frees us.

There is a disproportion between what we think about ourselves, between what we say about ourselves, and what in fact we are. What is the aim of our life?

We have to think, to understand where we want to arrive. Fifteen days before the exam, what is the motive for studying?

What is the motive for working? (Maybe it is not just a habit.) A decision in the present is required that cancels schemes and projects and, in the end, expresses itself as begging.

1) The goal is a begging.
2) The begging presupposes an esteem.
3) The esteem is not to be taken for granted.

Why do we live for a goal? To become familiar with that goal and to ask that it be present again.

The question, if it is true, is turned to the one who can give us life and supposes an esteem.

The esteem is not taken for granted. We need to decide in the present. How do we live a gesture in such a way that everything does not just pass away? How do we live our studies without losing anything? To live for a goal that remains, for a content that deepens in time. Each person has aims. The problem is to find the aim. To live in function of … gives strength to face the effort and a courage that we did not know before. It gives strength to open ourselves to life. How do we live the goal if not by begging? To live for a goal means to desire that Christ may intervene now. The goal promises me a comprehensive good. For this reason, we live for a goal. We need, therefore, to be very clear about what we are. To live for a goal is difficult. We need a daily vigilance, the passage from an implicit faith to an existential memory. Why or for whom do we study?

A day not lived for a goal is a day lost, in fact, lost because nothing remains. We need to be clear that the motive of our action is one. This motive emerges in a dramatic way, within a struggle that we often lose. The companionship exists so that we can help each other to conquer, to allow the suffocated voice to shout out. It is a struggle against worries. In front of the evidence of a miracle, anxiety is often more determinant.

I was able to experience the exam without worries, in the sense that the worry was a trampoline, a possibility to go beyond it. Because preoccupation about the exam causes distress, I am put in front of a crossroads: either I remain closed in the preoccupation about the exam, living the days of preparation in a heavy way, thinking only of the exam and closing myself to all the other stimuli, or I open myself to another measure. The latter option does not come naturally. I told myself every morning: this day is given for your growth. Within this faith, I have found freedom, the overcoming of anxiety. I was able to be thankful even for my preoccupations and for the other facts that did not enter into my measure, into what I wanted. There has also been a realism: the struggle for respect and for my studies. In the worry about the exam and about other things, I did not center my focus on the resolution of the problems; I did not ask myself, *How can I overcome them by my own strength?* but *How can I learn something definite for life starting from these unrepeatable moments?* Alternative: to map out the day starting from the worry, or to start from the fundamental need and to consider the worry as something to be confronted, as an announcement, as something that points beyond itself. The newness coincides with the truth of the situation. This is not newness in the intellectual sense, but in the sense of an openness of heart. The new coincides with the old, with that which touches the root of the person and waters it and reinforces it.

Realism and reasonableness to pursue efficiency and control of reality, to be positively set in motion, must remain within the environment of memory. In this sense, the insistence on memory and on the passage from the Movement as a horizon to the Movement as a breath of life is positive. We see a person engaged deep down when he reaches a capacity of judgment and can handle things both privately and publicly. The step of efficiency then cannot but be personal. It is certainly not just a matter of organization.

Memory is not something mystical, but an energy that opens to things and helps us to consider them in all their elements and to act accordingly.

Doesn't everyone think that the ideal should be real in some way? Or that it should have a foundation? Starting from a very practical point, my choice of career field is the fruit of searching for the answers to the desires that are common also for other men. These desires, appreciated, individualized, seeking an answer for their intimate nature, have found that answer in the encounter with an Other that is the resolution of existential problems. Having experienced the advantage of this choice, of this encounter that fills every action or every intention or every choice with meaning, I do not want my work simply to be conditioned by this encounter but determined by it. Now, because of the good things that are transmitted, my only concern is to witness to a new existential dimension, the Christian dimension, that is the Answer to man's desire for liberation. An engagement of a political character is valid for me, interesting, in the measure in which it is an occasion for the spreading of the Kingdom. An engagement that is absolutely mental does not interest me, that is, an engagement only of information or enthusiasm. It must have its own specificity, that is, be a carrier of values. We must discuss the *how* of this engagement.

Anxiety

Anxiety is caused by the fact that your heart is not with Christ but with something else. In fact, if your heart were with Christ, it would be at peace because He is there. He does not leave. He cannot leave. Instead, the heart is anxious because it is centered on what is unstable. You plunge into the horizon of instability when you try to resolve something with your own cunning, when you want to reach something with your own calculations. There are two sins in this case:

—You love a finite reality more than the stable Good.

—You count on yourself and do not trust the one who directs your life.

In the Movement, to entrust yourself means to ask.

To introduce a new term (Christ) that is not something intellectual, but a present and recognized fact. But where is this present and recognized fact? We know where a friend is, where our mother is, but what and where is this fact that should be introduced in our life? This fact is the substance of the companionship, is the face that becomes clear within a fabric of relationships, is that which is immediately perceived, phenomenologically perceived within a companionship.

The School of Community speaks about a place where the faithful gaze on things and on events is already a real attitude. Never before this period has this place been so close to me, so immanent. I experienced the Movement in Naples as something extraneous to me, as a weight, moralistically: I was doing things not because they had to do with my life in its entirety. The gestures I was doing involved only the moral and moralistic aspect of my person. (In spite of this moralism, I was changing.)

I do not believe I have completely overcome this attitude, but I am certain that, naturally, being in a way simpler (which does not mean easier), that is, with attention, with people, in a fabric of human relationships, things begin to change even when I am alone in front of a book. In the patience of expectation, I start to consider these gestures as if they were something that belongs to me. I am fostering a personal interest. In this case, the fact that, inexplicably, unexpectedly, people turn their gaze on me assumes a supremely important role. It is a strange gaze because it touches my life in all its aspects. It would have never crossed my mind to join the particular together with a meaning, if it had not been for this companionship, the place of the cultural event. This is so true that where this place does not exist, there is no longer a present judgment on the circumstances.

In our faculty, there have been two attempts at an assembly on the part of a *collective*. My attitude in front of these events and, in general, in front of the facts of the budget has not been completely passive. I presented myself at the assemblies with the intention of speaking, even if there was no need. There is maturing in me, an attention in front of things: the will to live with my head held high at the university. I desire to have power over my life and not just to put up with things. These desires have been reawakened in me by this companionship: on my own I would not have had the capacity to dream nor the strength to think of and do these things. The greatest danger is to consider these things as obvious, to enter again into the normality of the Movement, not to feel it all as a gift. The Movement is something exceptional, because only in this place have I felt the things that I have said.

A new step

1) What has animated me in these months has been the desire for human growth that, among other things, has made me face the difficulties that for a while I have held within: an embarrassment within the Movement. This desire has become a question, spoiled sometimes by forgetting what I truly need, seeking instead to defend an artificial image and a role. Other times, the question has been spoiled by a laziness and a weakness, like when I let fear prevent me from opening up and living intensely the *extraneous* circumstances.

2) This question did not fall into nothing, but found a ground or even a response. It does not concern only the initial, intuitive response, but also an answer that I find along the way. There has been first a positive content and then the resurgence of the question. The content of my self-awareness is not only the question, but also the support that I have found in a few people who still accompany me.

3) These people have fostered an esteem for the Movement that was generated by a clear initial intuition. This deep

esteem—for a gift received—is very strong and has made me accept many difficulties that otherwise I would not have faced. Now there is an openness toward understanding the path to follow in order for this esteem to become something existential.

Belonging is the awareness of being looked at (in a strong sense) and welcomed by someone who has given us what we have and can give us even more. Adhesion to the companionship means adhesion to what fills our life. Otherwise, we belong through a moralistic mechanism (as happens today for many).

Gratitude is the measure of the heart of one who belongs: I am nothing; everything has been given to me. It is an open and joyful dimension of the person. But if everything has been given to me, in order to become stronger I have to ask for it.

Everything happens in peace: I am guided. Ultimately, I am not alone. We need something that is solid and stable. We have met something that is solid and stable. Hope is founded on a certain presence. My expectation of desired results is not hope. Our day is either the expectation of the next step that must come or it is the tension to take as much as we can from the present that we have in hand.

What gives the strength to withstand the circumstances, the continual weaknesses that come up, and to accept them, is only the expectation of a result (tomorrow these circumstances will be overcome). If I did not have this hope, I would die under the adversities that come up. Instead, the weaknesses and adversities point forward to the better thing that is prepared for us: that Christ will show Himself. Everything calls me to a hope that is founded on the fact that today I am better than yesterday (therefore, a change is possible), and also on the fact that the day that I am living might be even greater. This is what I desire. But all of this happens in a true place. Tomorrow, I will set up our Communion and Liberation table, but I will not do it in the usual way. I am looking to grow from my daily work. (This is the hope that Christ will show Himself in every circumstance of life, even the most familiar.)

The Movement is not a bunch of things to do, nor is it a series of thoughts to understand; it is rather the place where you live and where you express the deepest desire that you are, that constitutes you. You are a desire for fulfillment. The sign that you await something is evident in the dissatisfaction that you carry within, in the perception that life could be more intense and more true. We are lacking the existential feeling of belonging, that is, the true awareness of our I, that we belong to an Other. This lack makes our hope stumble. Our hope is not founded on a certain fact—the content of the encounter we have had, that has touched the deepest level of our I—but on a childish emotiveness. Hope must be founded above all on the awareness of belonging to a mercy, to a stable support that guides your steps. Then it is founded on the certainty of the change, inasmuch as, in the past, a change has happened. It is founded on a present desire.

Every School of Community is meant to put us again in front of what we have encountered.

1) There are limits that we tend to censure. We must become aware of the limit in order to be born again. This aspect must not be censured.

2) We live the relationship with the limit in a way that we prefer to remain in the quicksand; we love the limit that we are. *I am the things that happen.* Instead, one should ask the reason why. There is a Satanic temptation in us, to fall in love with the limit that we are: *it is secure; the next time it will be better.* The center that we have found makes our whole life move.

3) One learns only if one has a relationship that judges according to truth, a truth that respects the deepest need that we are. We need to be clear about this need that we are, helped by a guide.

4) A personal problem emerges: you must choose what you want to be. To ask is to establish a relationship with the one who guides you now and who gives you energy now.

I do not really believe that Tuesday[7] is the living place in which I put my life in play. I still think that my life is in play within the traditional schemes that have damaged my heart. There is a scheme: traditional Christianity. I think more about what I have in my head than about the place where I am flourishing. There is a great reticence to put into play that ultimate part of myself. I have arrived where I have never arrived before: to put even my reticence into play. Will I be faithful to this task? Almost everyone among us arrives at a point beyond which he does not go. I have always believed in Tuesday, but too distantly. I have always followed my own points for meditation, not those of Tuesday. Or at least I have placed the two side by side. But it should not be like this. Everything comes from this. I am afraid to appear as I am: a shy man. But this is not how it should be. The community has already welcomed me for what I am.

The Movement is for me something extra, a distraction. Deep down, this objection has not yet disappeared completely.

Encounter

Through the formation I've received, I have grown in the Movement with the awareness that deep down it was not only here that my life was in play. The discovery of these last days is precisely this: the companionship to which I belong is the living place where it is possible to become familiar with the content of the faith, the only reality that has completely corresponded to me. A few times, my soul has awakened and has looked ahead starting from the present fact, which is the content of the companionship. Other times, it is as if I did not have this full vigilance, and thus the circumstances easily overpower me, because in many respects I am still weak. Above all, when there is this vigilance of which I

---

7. He is referring to the meetings for preparing the School of Community.

spoke before, in facing studies, at our Communion and Liberation table, in relationships with friends, the point of departure is clear to me, the direction I should follow is clear to me, what I should expect, what I should hope for is clear. Despite the confusion that sometimes is created in my mind, I desire quite reasonably to draw closer to the one who can make me better. The difficulty and the struggle that I am living (I will just mention one) is this: the will to be respected by certain friends is strong in me. This preoccupation distances me from the object of my hope, does not let me employ all my energy for the one essential thing. Anyway, I can live both the expectation and the difficulties within a fact that is certain and is already present, so certain and so present as to have accompanied and to accompany me with a surprising constancy. One thing is to hope vaguely, another to hope starting from a stable fact, that is, a reality encountered, verified and gradually matured. This fact marks out the path; it is the criterion with which to face things.

1) What I want is to attach myself with certainty to what corresponds to me. It is already present, and I hope that it becomes ever more so.

2) The hope of becoming familiar with the content of the Christian experience has led me to strain, and that is still there but it is lessening. To accept a friendship that has been proposed to me, to overcome all the embarrassment and all the inexplicable barriers—this has been and is the motive for which I live the gestures of the community.

3) It is also the point of departure that gives order to my days. For example, becoming familiar with the Movement leads to a time of study that is intelligent. Either one studies to finish the program or one studies to understand (and in this second case accomplishes also the first). After the encounter, there is a series of projects for their own sake. The difficulty is how to connect the encounter with these many projects. This connection is vocation.

1) Either the projects do not impact life understood in the light of elementary experience or 2) we insist that the encounter illuminate immediately the particular (the particular project). The *problem*: that I may finally be myself. In what way does this love influence things? One way, for example, is the fact that I immediately return to what I am living, beyond the contingent difficulties; if this present experience is not there, my hope is frustrated. Certainty is founded on what is already true and on the change that we have seen, to equip ourselves to face things (study, the things we don't understand, etc.).

The Church as the "place" of regeneration
There is in me the desire to go back always to the essential level, the elementary point of departure. I would like for everything—encounters, conversations, difficulties—to be occasions for going back to that level. I would like every action and every word to start from that level. At this level, there is a fact that does not allow me to succumb in front of adversities, because it overcomes them, giving them a meaning. This place of authenticity frees me from everything (anxieties, things to do, judgment from others). I belong to everything. Ordinarily, though, it is not like this because certain ghosts prevail:

1) disordered thoughts that direct me to the past, to the future, to the probable, to the fantastic, to the hypothetical, and distract me from the present which alone is;
2) a series of personal projects linked to a logic of power: the worries of life (the absence of a step forward from the Movement, a sign that its content is true. This leap forward is the passage from the logic of the group to personal awareness).

Put in play, this month, what we have encountered, with the desire to come out of the month changed. In other words, the passage from a general respect for the Movement to a visible expression of myself. Only a certainty, a companionship (the support that this gives) can give the audacity we need, despite the weakness that one has. What is the reason that in this moment convinces us to adhere to the experience we have had?

1) There is in me a solid respect for the Movement.
2) The problem is that this respect is generic; it does not become a decision in the present (in study, at our CL table). I work at our table. I do it also for the Movement, but in the present there is not a pressing question or, better, sometimes there is, and sometimes there isn't. If you do not go to the depth with the other, you do not reach the depth of yourself. My life is a gift; it cannot be spent just wasting time. The Movement has taught me to live fully even in the banality of life.

The reason I am here is that this is the only place where, in an evident way, we speak about ourselves simply, but at the level of the person that is the root of everything. I do not speak simply about my characteristics, my ideas, my future, etc., but about what is deepest in all this. I am here for another motive: because of a natural need for companionship, which here is founded on what I said before, a companionship in the depths of the person, which the others bring out. My difficulties are linked to my incapacity to pass from understanding that the level of the heart is what counts, to a present attention to what I am saying. Should I tell you about my days? It is true, deep down there is peace, connected to a companionship. Over this layer of peace there is the daily anxiety to do six hours of study, and above all a lack of energy and coherence to live in the present. The sensibility with which I live things has certainly grown with respect to before, but there is also nostalgia for some brief periods in the past which were characterized by an attention to things, by a taste for studies, etc., that now are no longer there. It is a vague, involuntary laziness, which I overcome through an exercise of my intellect and will, without enthusiasm.

Joyful Days Ahead

There is the possibility, at every moment, to put yourself again in a position of loyalty. When we are loyal deep down, we recognize it. This recognition is accompanied by peace. When loyalty is not there, you can fail to recognize the point and proceed without ever getting it. The point is to live at the level of the heart; if we do not arrive there, the Movement still has not truly touched us. But we understand this only if we have had an experience of that level. Either we face reality starting from that level, or the difference between us and the Communists or the DC[8] is only a question of political intelligence. Reality is an open possibility; we can close ourselves to this to the point of mapping out our own lives starting from the thoughts that torment our head. There is the possibility to live reality with dignity (dignity is an attention to the constitutive demands of your being; otherwise what is our dignity?). The Movement has opened our hearts and has thrown us into life.

A judgment on everything, starting from elementary needs

This School of Community is the possibility, among other things, to grow in the awareness of what I am living; this fuller awareness signals a step forward. I have gained a greater awareness of what has allowed me to move forward so quickly in these months, what for me has been decisive. It has been a judgment on things, a judgment expressed both of those things that I was about to do and of those things that I had done. The judgment is the emergence of your person in front of reality. It is starting from what you are deep down, which is a need to be loved and thus to find correspondence to your desire. From this comes the strength to face life.

At the university, in Naples, a place where the majority of people are gradually worn out, I have happened to grow. Reality, objectively fragile, becomes a place of correspondence if you start from your elementary experience. Reality has not only not blocked desire, it has sustained desire, providing for it a field of action. In these last days, the most important passage has transpired, from a conception of the Movement as a horizon in which one lives,

8. The Christian Democrat Party.

a horizon of friends, of gestures, of things that fill up your day (sometimes too much), a reassuring place, to a conception of the Movement as an event that gives life to a personal movement, which for example has shaped a freedom in front of an exam at which I myself am amazed. But the freedom in my studies is possible only when I live for a goal other than study; thus, anxiety does not consume my days. Putting in play the truest part of ourselves, which in general is suffocated within things, we begin to change the gaze that we have on the Movement: the place where desire emerges in its depth, together with the initial vision of an efficacious response, which changes life (and has already changed it).

One of the characteristic aspects of the Movement is the consideration of human need, a consideration that gradually gets forgotten after one has made a choice for faith. This forgetfulness is common for many Catholics. Our attempt is to highlight human need, reminding ourselves of the need for witnesses. Here, in Benevento, there isn't yet a point of reference like at the University of Naples, the political Popular Movement,[9] understood as a commitment toward the outside world, something done as a group. However, there is the hope that, individually, there is flourishing in everyone the love toward this new fact that has been given to us, and in consequence the will to help others also participate in the Christian experience.

Certainly, it would be great now to find a way to begin a common action, a Popular Movement in fact, convinced as we are, at least theoretically (but it is not enough to be theoretical), that only if we live Christianity fully do we perceive existence with a new energy. In fact, to the extent that we, as individuals and as a group, are able to draw near to the ideal, we perceive the beauty of life. If testimony diminishes among us, we are not faithful to anything. We were not chosen because we were more beautiful, but because

---

9. This is an independent political initiative started with an inspiration from the charism of Communion & Liberation. There are other similar independent initiatives like AVSI and the Meeting of Rimini.

we must carry to an unhappy world a joyful message, the possibility of a better life.

The involvement in the university that was entrusted to me by friends, publicizing the elections, things which are only a pretext for encountering people, are gradually changing me. It is true, as has been said, that when we think about great things, about our witness, the small problems disappear. The personal experience of friendship can be characterized by a double aspect: on one hand, the *normal* relationships, those which characterize the man who is thrown into the world of inauthenticity. These relationships have something true about them (because otherwise we would be completely degraded) and something false. The second aspect of friendship is what is lived even among people who are strangers to this *truth*. This is paradoxical: people that we might not know may live the greatest friendship, friendship in community. A reality is revealed by its action. Barking reveals the dog. A book reveals what is behind a man. A friendship without ulterior motives, such that not even spouses find, reveals something super-human. To have encountered this Reality should mean that we conserve it always, that we desire it, that we choose it when dilemmas come. In the measure in which the Mystery of the community deepens, we desire this new companionship.

The beginning of fulfillment of what you desire (the Kingdom): this is the Movement. When we find a new Fact, the answer touches us deeply; in an instant, we understand that this is the road. We walk without hurry and without hesitation, because that instant becomes a fact that directs every moment of our existence.

The order to be built

There is, every day, the possibility to build an order with our own hands. Such a construction, though, has as its principle and end, as its cause and completion, something that is beyond human strength. We move within grace, in a horizon that does not coincide with ours, but that is always extended beyond. And yet within this horizon that is not exhausted by our awareness, there is the possibility to build the *new* and then to contemplate it. Our enthusiasm, that is, our familiarity with the divine, depends on the contemplation of something that needs our creativity in order to be built. The *work* involves everything in man, personally, and makes him feel like a participant in reality. Daily, either we are builders of the beautiful or we are a part of the forces that lead to desperation. Study, for example, should be done not only efficiently, but beautifully; beauty contains efficiency (as a prize that was not sought).

The level of the "further on"

There exists a level of nature in the relationship with things that has gone missing. Nihilism is the ultimate outcome of the consumption of things. When we do not live in the world of life, different kinds of phantasms dominate. The phantasms are at the level of excessive abstraction. The relationship between two people, when it does not proceed on the existential level, is false. That relationship, instead, must serve to throw us into life, to descend into that dimension of concreteness made of physicality and of unveiling our soul without shame. The long road to the recovery of meaning passes through a re-evaluation of the particular, of the instant that we live, of the word that we pronounce. Only a perspective that saves the particular can avoid the dissolution of things. Moving forward into unexplored regions of the *further on*, through putting into play what is normally hidden by excessive formalities or by calming gestures, is the first step toward the recovery of the self. The authentic recovery of the self means being surprised at one's own existence, which in the end boils down to an expectation of meaning. That meaning, though, is further on, ungraspable, always further. Being inexhaustible and unknowable, the meaning makes everything that we encounter inexhaustible and never totally knowable. The crisis of the contemporary world is about not clinging to the materiality of life, taking refuge in a comfortable zone of obviousness where everything is calculated, everything is controlled, everything is decided and directed. We sense that, if we recover the particular, we re-open the perspective of a symbolic gaze on reality. This is possible despite the fact that Heidegger affirms that constitutively we live in the "oblivion of being."

The heart of the Church

The *social* turn in Christianity distorts the Church. This means turning the life of the Church toward activism, worrying ourselves excessively about the interpretation of history in order to elaborate plans of redevelopment and things of this sort; or to obstinantly seek out the structural causes of humanity's woes and to expend ourselves in a sociological effort. All this is the ruin of the Church. In the less grave cases it is like a veil that covers the face; in other cases, it is a Church robbed of her nature. Deep down, man is not interested in a socially avant-garde Church that resolves problems or exercises power wherever problems appear. This is not the heart of the Church. People remain indifferent in front of a Church that occupies itself with problems, setting aside *the* problem; people are tired of hearing the Church speak about everything but the person. A sociological Church, that is founded on the interpretation of history and on recipes for re-constructing society, always goes together with ideology. It is one cultural *position* among so many others. But Jesus Christ, when He descended to earth, encountered people by proposing something different for them, not a program but the only path that leads to the fulfillment of life. *The* problem is the meaning of life: the Church must announce this. The rest is legitimate if it starts from and is in harmony with this heart.

The handicap of bourgeois-ism

The life of the handicapped must not generate only an emotional gasp of compassion. The handicapped are the sign that makes us comprehend that reality is bigger than what we think. There exists in fact a dimension within which these lacks are, I don't say accidental, but positive, instruments to move forward. We must acquire familiarity with a dimension that includes also these things, seeing that the ordinary perspective from which we start, and within which we move, tends to censure these phenomena or, in the best cases, to consider them negative accidents that nature has produced, unfortunate cases that we try to make the best of, the best being understood in a bourgeois way. The dominant mentality expresses a vision of the world that leaves many lingering questions.

Bourgeois-ism and power (the height of the caricature)

Bourgeois-ism is the absence of the dramatic sense of existence; its outcome is the obsessive and almost maniacal will to grasp power. In fact, the absence of the dramatic sense of existence coincides with the shelving of the true image of man, a being that awaits total fulfillment. From this setting aside there arises a caricature, the greatest caricature of the true man: the one who seeks the realization of the self through power, the satisfaction of pride. But life is more than that.

Christianity

The absence of *Christianity* is not an imperfection to be noticed in the face of an existing metaphysical model. The absence of *Christianity* disturbs us not because *morality is disappearing*. The absence of Christianity is the lack of an objective horizon, of an edifying environment, of a climate that breathes. But the gods have fled the world. A part of us is not involved. "And everything agrees not to speak of us."[10]

Technological society

Man has conquered the world but has lost his soul, his identity, his belonging to a reality that gives him a face and a consistency (the face is the expression of a consistency; consistency is given by the connection to a strong reality that defines man in his thoughts and in his actions).

---

10. "And everything agrees not to speak of us, half out/of shame, maybe, and half out of ineffable hope." Rainer Maria Rilke, *Duino Elegies*, Elegy 2, vv. 42–44.

Life and theology

The individual religious dynamic, intuition-experience, is reproduced in the history of Christianity. Our intuition is the epoch of biblical revelation, and the period of the Fathers is our experience, our work of deepening, rediscovery, and development of the already-given richness. Theology, if it is not this, is chit-chat. The richness of theology is in fact all at the beginning, and its novelty has ancient roots. The novelty that did not already exist is vanity, and vain is the modern man who chases after novelty.

To propose secular humanism as a universal vision of the world—in the sense that it can welcome into itself different tendencies, including Christianity (in order to do this it is enough to put transcendence in parentheses and insist on those values that are contained also in the humanistic conception)—is the most intelligent attempt (that is becoming fully successful) to secularize the world without anyone putting up any obstacles to this action. That this attempt may succeed fully is demonstrated by the fact that modern Catholics are completely integrated in the world. They believe in peace, in equality, in freedom, as these things are proposed by the secular culture. This culture can count on modern Catholics who step aside democratically in order to permit practically everything.

Those who do not teach certainty do not show impartiality but, rather, teach a wrong certainty: that there are no certainties. From this arises the superficial attitude of many towards the problem of truth, which is not considered an important problem precisely because they have not been taught certainty.

Without criteria, man is a helpless spectator of a multiplicity of events without connection. For this reason, there is an impression of dizziness and not of comprehension.

The Church must return to being the place where man feels the words that touch him most closely.

Only through the experience of faith, of authority, of risk, of following, can we see the saints as the existential models that have preceded us.

We reacquire roots through openness to the call and through feeling that which distinguishes the life of our true fathers.

The divine law—which is secure—obliges us to follow the way that leads to happiness. In fact, we cannot imagine a God that would want us to be unhappy. For this reason, if He tells us to give witness to Him, He does so because by giving witness we find ourselves, we are better, even if the law is uncomfortable.

However strange it may seem, given that from every side the opposite is affirmed, freedom cannot be identified with free will. We will be tempted to set these two concepts against each other (as Donoso Cortés affirms, "free will, far from being the presupposition of freedom, is a danger for it"), but neither is this the right way to follow. We explain first of all that with the term *freedom* the Catholic tradition has always indicated that state of perfection where man finds himself when he is unchained from passion and from "the things of this world" and when his distance from God is minimal. This is right because we do not think there is a term more appropriate to indicate a state of soul so sublime. Perfection is reached with the will (necessarily guided and supported by supernatural means).

To understand a general principle, it is much easier if one starts from simple, practical examples. In front of the problem of divorce, the position is well known of those who, while rejecting divorce on principle, did not think it right to prohibit it or take away the possibility from those who were of a contrary opinion, out of respect for their free will. Given that no one wants to deny free will, which the most terrible and efficacious dictator could not eliminate, we throw a deeper gaze on the question. Reason and experience suggest that we oppose positions that are only apparently wise (as the wolves of which the Gospel speaks are only apparently docile), for the basic reason that, once divorce is accepted and practiced as normal, once it does not appear as something new, different, and unscrupulous, it will become the horizon set by those who want to subvert Christian morality. And instead of turning ourselves to God, the human mind will direct itself more and more to the "world" (as happened).

If Christianity were only an idea, the point would be nihilistic abstraction, philosophical sin. But Christianity deals with facts.

It is clear that for one who experiences order in its multiple manifestations, the temptation to deny it does not appear. One who denies order does it to turn his moral baseness into an intellectual problem. Nihilism is the philosophical version of sin: the codification of the absurd.

Matrimony is the answer to man's desire for stability, understood in an Augustinian way.

A point of research: the passion of love is the sign of the absolute love that man must have for God. This passion is often, when taken to the extreme, a substitution for the authentic love of God.

Sin is a step backward. Temptation is the possibility of a step forward.

The university, like never before, needs a stable action, one with a firm foundation. But what makes this possible? Certainly not the call to generic objectives, in which we lose the concreteness of the daily event, nor in projects that deliberate on the perfect reform of the school (nor the tired call to the forms of political initiative that, trying on paper to protect the rights of everyone, sacrifice them to the ideological wishes of the few). A stable action needs first of all reasons that stand up in front of reality in all its aspects (the evil of the university is much deeper than that underlined in these months in the various protests), that push us to give answers to the various needs that we encounter. The crisis of political activity in these years and the consequent skepticism, which led to a kind of *every man for himself*, is born from a way of facing reality where the space is not filled in between those who call themselves *the collective*, the *social*, the *public*, and the experience of the individual. Free spaces, where each person, with his own identity, can develop humanly significant relationships, where examples of change are already tangible, are the most concrete place where we can begin to develop a movement.

"...Dreaming of systems so perfect that no one will need to be good."[11]

Christianity

All the arguments that are used to denigrate Christianity, from a philosophical point of view and from a historical, theological point of view should be interpreted honestly by the Christian, because certainly they will consolidate and will not destroy Christianity (holy wars, claims to truth, plurality of truths, etc.). The conflict between different creeds has happened because there will always be conflicts, as long as there are people. In these situations, you want to leave a mark. Life is worth something. In a skeptical epoch, a time of *tolerance*, there will always be conflict, but it will not help anyone; rather, it will only be harmful. It is false to say that **certainty** generates **intolerance** and thus **war**.

The need to overcome regret finds expression in Hegel's *everything that is real is rational* and its complement in the Christian principle that God knows how to bring a greater good out of any evil that He permits. But in any case, the regret remains.

We do not concede that it is impossible to go beyond the scope commonly defined by the sensible. Why base ethics on the destruction of values as if it could be demonstrated that no foundation, no norm exists? Perception can be common or uncommon. It can be relative or non-relative. Sensibility, that is, the perception of something tangible, is a concept that changes according to the times. Sensibility, in this era, is very limited.

Truth is verified through the comparison of different planes. It should harmonize everything. To affirm that truth is not reachable

---

11. T.S. Eliot, *Choruses from "The Rock,"* VI.

is the fruit of considerations that have not been preceded by an authentic engagement. To affirm that the truth, if it exists, must be intuitable and immediately evident is a misunderstanding of nature, which allows itself to be conquered only if we put in the effort. In order to eat, we must work; the truth is a difficult conquest, but it is possible.

We desire to feel ourselves on the side of the good.

We do not need to believe ourselves immediately able to overcome the formalism of certain cultural acts. Just as the Law has a function of direction and finds its fulfillment in the law of the Spirit, which includes it and overcomes it (in the sense that it makes us not feel the weight of the precept), so also certain forms guide, but the goal of these forms is elsewhere. Let us proceed with constancy and patience, which sooner or later will arrive at the goal, which is to live certain forms fully, even with our heart, not only with our reason.

The essential content of these pages, as far as regards morality, is this: our relationships with others, our passions, our interests, our capacities, have a foundation that, not dealing with it, not assuming it as a point of departure for a work of intelligence and will, makes everything vain and becomes artificial in relationships (trying to present ourselves to others in ways that are not true), and only feeds a mask that does not have positive features.

The desire that in this moment should bring us together consists in putting ourselves in front of the event we have encountered, the presentiment of new life that we have had, personally. You have encountered a companionship in which stories are told, experiences of change. You continue to come here because at least you do not feel totally distant from what we tell each other. You feel that it could have something to do with you. From afar you intuit that it is not false. In short, there is a reason why you come. This reason needs to be looked at in the face; we need to say *You* to the content present in our friendship (the content is the answer to the question, *What binds us in the end?*). *Who do you say that I am*: this goes outside of the logic of the group. Your person must emerge, your face must express the outlines that it has, because the Creator does great things, which then become small because of your laziness, because of your complications, because of your envy. You have these outlines because you have a place where you are guided to search for your face (we need humility to accept the support, otherwise we remain outside of life).

—But what is your support deep down, that is, the content of your personal awareness? We have encountered something that holds everything: Christ, encountered in the apparent banality of the circumstances. God does nothing by chance. We have encountered something that claims to be everything in your life, to determine your thoughts and your actions. The Beauty that exists should enter everywhere and inform all of our time; we must learn to remember the Event, to put ourselves again in front of what has happened, that is giving shape to what happens.

—The result is a reassuring tranquility. You get up calm in the morning because, in the depth of the perspective with which you see things, from people to the food you eat, you see His Presence.

> I lie prostrate in the dust (*Psalm* 119:25).
> I cry out in sadness (*Psalm* 119:28).
> The Lord will sustain him on this bed of pain (*Psalm* 41:4).
> Make the effort to be considered as nothing.

> Pride (to be a banner in front of others)
> Perfectionism which makes everything crumble

What gives us security is the memory of what we have seen. The Spirit that has been given to us is not a spirit of timidity.
   —Culture is the expression.

Culture of belonging and culture of emancipation

V. Metz, to define the mentality of man that arose after the Middle Ages, lingers on the term *emancipation*. Since the end of the Middle Ages up to our day, a criterion of judgment and action has prevailed: the liberation from bonds, of whatever type these may be. We can subscribe fully to a similar interpretation of historical evolution, all the more so since we are helped, calling on a single concept, to understand indepth phenomena that are apparently different, but derived from one root. In what sense do we talk about a culture of belonging? We came upon the introduction to a series of historical studies on medieval man, made by Le Goff. According to the noted historian, medieval man had a model of life toward which he tended. This model is found in *Genesis*, a book that, through a narration, shows the created nature of man. To affirm that man is a creature, who depends on an Other, is not so harmless to say today. To say *man is a creature* means to fluster centuries of Western history. The theoretical value of such an expression—man is a creature—is clarified in relation to the method by which we reach an affirmation of this type. That is, if we want to understand the essence of something, we must begin by observation in the present and then go to the origins for proof, to look at the rock from which we are extracted. The essence that makes man essentially what he is and not another (here the ontological and the ethical plane overlap) is in his origin from another. Preceding man, there is something from an Other, which is the reason for man's existence. Having said this, we understand the moral necessity of living according to such a truth, as a dependent creature and not as the master of things.

*There is a type of collective experience that believes it is able to grasp all good things. Space and time are limited. I want everything and I want it now. To want to have an experience that tests everything is the mark of an **open-type of person**.

*There is the alternative of placing our whole person in a single good. "When you are happy with a girl, or with any other particular, you begin to be afraid." This is the mark of a **closed-type of person**.

*It is beginning to be true for some of us that *we need to seek one thing in order to find everything*. There is a central point of human experience, as there is a central point in a plant, which is the seed.

Everything is contained within that point. There is the ultimate development. In man, this is called the heart, which is underground, in the unconscious. Yet it exists and it has to be awakened to begin to live. If the heart lives, everything is saved, everything is a good.

*Power arrives to make us take care of our branches, that is, our interests, which then are without roots. We lose gusto. When there is self interest, it is accompanied by an absence of liberty.

*The Encounter, through the companionship, awakens the heart because the Lord of the heart is present.

We are characterized by an extreme positivity. What is better than an Event that proposes to you a perspective within which everything is saved? Even the obscurity of the instant that passes is illuminated by a new light.

The Particular serves the whole

*Point in common: the loss of the meaning of things, of the value of use. In a car, the wheel serves the whole; in the body, the hand serves the person. Thus, the good that you find serves your destiny.

To reawaken the **memory** means to have a **true** gaze on reality. It is to go beyond everyday life; it is the contrary of an illusion. We do not need to hide ourselves in a utopia or in the imagination to dream about a good world for us. We need to dispel the cloud that is in front of our eyes in order to see good, in order to behold the positivity that exists objectively. The positivity that exists is the Companionship that has said "follow and you will change," and this is what happened. This positivity exists because the change is a sign of the presence of a Force that moves things. To live in the memory of this means to keep vigil, to be men. Man is characterized by the search for meaning; that Force is the Meaning of life. Man is rational. He is vigilant when he exercises reason, when it is an **activity**. Memory is an **activity**.

Joyful Days Ahead

Reason is openness. It is not the creator. Contradiction is the contrast between the expectation of the infinite of man and what the ideologies propose. They propose something that, to be affirmed, must eliminate certain elements, certain component parts of man. Aside from our faith, which is often too traditional, we still ask ourselves: What do I really want? What is my expectation? I can imagine the best for my future, but the expectation that constitutes me is not satisfied, is not filled. What do I await? What is my expectation? It is the expectation of newness. The hundredfold is a newness. It is not what I have in mind. Otherwise, I fall into my own limits again. I remain stagnant, wrapped up in myself. This is not the way to decenter myself. I am exceedingly sensitive to the things that happen around me. As if I myself am at the center; this *I* needs to be lost. Decentering means that I don't think, closed in my limits, about what would be good for me. In prayer, I ask for what the community tells me to seek. The hundredfold is the opening up in front of me of perspectives and realities that I did not imagine before. Happiness is not the realization of my personal project. It is the gift that reveals itself as newness. In this sense, no one knows where his happiness is, in what it consists. Happiness is an encounter. This mental structure that should be created is the only one that can help me in my studies. It is at the basis of culture. We need to lose ourselves in order to find ourselves. Expectation is the expectation of new heavens and a new earth; we need to have a foretaste of them now.

1) Ordinarily, the things that we have in front of us are an obstacle. Reality is that the Fact is represented in the circumstances. So the problem is you; it is a problem of your attitude (not something moralistic) in front of things.

2) The drama of affection consists in belonging to something different from yourself. To belong is not spontaneous. Instinctive affection takes place without problems. The affection we are talking about here is different. It is the facing of opposite aspects. The other is different, not how you imagine him.

3) The drama is when you are struck by something. You have to take note of it. You cannot reduce it. Everything is for this.

4) Affection is arid when it does not pass through things that are different from you. Without obstacles, we become arid, resigned. We have often been reduced in this way. Something has struck us and has marked our life; the drama is to recognize this encounter always.

The Church as the place of the unveiling of humanity
— The distance between the image and what is.
— In the horizon of mercy (which gives shape to spaces in our life), a drama unfolds.
— In order to find ourselves, we must be in a companionship with all our intelligence and affection.
— Affection is the state of soul provoked by belonging to something.
—Man, in order to realize himself, must belong to the project of salvation, but he privileges his dreams.
—An inexorable direction has to do with breathing, with living like you were in front of destiny.

Elements of the Drama
The encountered Reality everything is for this impact with reality.

February 3, 1984
The only goal we should pursue, consciously or not (in this second case, by reason of a rational decision that accompanies the mind also when it does not think directly about the end), is to try to hold fast better and better to the covenant. As it has been said: "Everything lives *only* by desiring to love you more closely" (Jacopone da Todi). Here is the absolute exclusivity of our action. Outside of this, there is nothing else.

February 8, 1984

Letter to the Romans 3:9–26
It is clear in the first part that the *just one* in the absolute sense does not exist, and that because of the evil that everyone commits, everyone would be condemned according to the law. If we hope to save ourselves by virtue of the initiative of our individual will, we delude ourselves. We are all guilty in front of the law. Salvation comes from redemption and the *just one* is saved because of faith. Faith is the recognition of this fact, that is, of human weakness and thus of a total surrender to God. Perfectionism and scrupulosity are the denial of human weakness, the negation of the first point. Because of this they deny the second, the surrender to God. Scrupulosity is man's attempt to be perfect in front of the law of God.

February 10, 1984

A fundamental aspect of morality is this: not to make a step that is longer than the leg. To feel the urgency of a duty without having the strength to carry it out is a situation that leads to anxiety. As in our studies, we learn a chapter after reading it many times. Thus, gradually, we are able to do what we, the time before, thought to be impossible. This is confirmed by divine pedagogy. And God knows man very well.

March 16, 1984

The invocation that introduces Morning Prayer—"O God, come to my assistance"—indicates the state in which man finds himself on this earth, even if he belongs to the faith. It is a precarious state , a state that requires a liberation, a salvation. We would not say "come to my assistance" if we did not need salvation. The precariousness is owing, before all else, to the imperfect freedom of man who has the possibility to distance himself from the way of salvation. Then this freedom does not immediately perceive the ultimate reality and thus does not endure the highs and lows of feeling linked to the encounter we have had.

March 18, 1984

The deepening of religious **feeling** is gained through the development of the way we feel everyday things, and music, and human affections, and aesthetic taste. The concept of analogy is fundamental—a concept expressed rationally by Saint Thomas, but already implicitly present in religious souls, who have always noticed the traces of the divine on this earth, which allows us to comprehend the essential religious sentiments. The deepening of our humanity leads to greater comprehension. For example, living in depth, as a child, the relationship with our own father, we accumulate experiences that rise up more easily to the characteristics of the divine fatherhood. The examples are innumerable (gratuitous love, suffering, humiliation, spiritual awakening).

March 29, 1984

Maybe the fundamental reason why, not even among faithful Catholics, are we able to find unity is the lack of desire to put our own opinions on questions of lesser importance to the side. Radical obedience hardly exists anymore.

April 6, 1984

Christian life is true in the measure that it repeats the divine gestures fulfilled in history. Mentality, knowledge, action, word—everything has a value only if it reproduces in miniature what has already been felt, done, said. The *gratuitous good* is the most important and meaningful example, above all today, in a world where relationships of self-interest reign among men.

April 7, 1984

No rejection of the world
When it is said that the earth where we live is a valley of tears, an exile, we must immediately consider the condition of man. This earth is an exile not because of the goods that it gives to man, the goods which are the first fruits of the goods that do not end, but because of the goods that are not there or at least are not perfectly

present. A small misfortune is enough to shake a man profoundly. This imperfection will not exist in the true homeland. The word homeland indicates a place where we find ourselves at ease, where we do not experience disorientation.

May 6, 1984

The importance of the awareness of what we feel comes from the force of the *impressions* that dominate the mind. We can overcome subjectivism if we consider the rock of comparison that is the tradition of the Church. Because it can be for us the comparison between what we feel and what the Church proposes as a model, it is indispensable to give a communicable, rational shape to what we feel. Meditation that aims to reach awareness of our experiences is the solid foundation on which to build the rest. The rest can be, for example, an emotional outburst. Self-awareness, which is founded on rationality—the comparison among our impressions and the doctrine of the Church is in fact rational—is comparable to the good wood that, alone, allows the fire to last. It is foolish to put straw on the fire—that is, superficial enthusiasm. It is foolish to want to burn the green wood, which is too hard, which is too legalistic, which is too scrupulous. Should we pay attention to what we feel as sinful or to what our teachers have taught us? Only the wood that is dried properly gets burned! Only that will give warmth! It is in this fire that disagreements are dissolved, not so much in the anxious search for the distinction between mortal and venial sin.

May 23, 1984

Saint Phillip Neri invited us to keep scrupulosity and melancholy far from us. The mentality of the scrupulous, beyond being harmful to the self, is also productive of false dramas at the community level.

— With regard to the personal sphere, we must remember the duty to love ourselves, because even in our own soul the image of God is present. As we defend ourselves instinctively from enemies, thus we need to defend ourselves against the enemies that live within us together with the normal and good tendencies.

— Scrupulosity is damaging from the communal point of view in so far as it blocks communication.

— At the intellectual level, it generates integralist positions (in the negative sense of the term): the incapacity to listen to others and above all the anxiety to say the whole truth when it would be better just to say part of it. When we are presented with *absolutes* accompanied by anxiety, we are looking at a case of neurosis.

— The integral growth of the human person passes through the overcoming of these warped and twisted forms of religiosity, forms that have led many to study the religious phenomenon as a form of pathology. The witness of integral health that depends on experience of the sacred is of the greatest importance in an epoch troubled by anguish, fear, and neurosis.

May 23, 1984

The force of gravity that man experiences every day, and that powerfully conditions even our worship, has been tamed in Christianity. Unlike pagan peoples, who from a probable initial monotheism attached themselves to idolatry, in Christianity this risk is avoided. Worship must be directed to a man, to a reality in a certain way perceptible to the senses. Such is the grace given, such is the gravity of a violation. Idolatry cannot stand up to examination. The dead, the saints, and the angels, mediators—all these complement the Christian reality, a reality with the characteristics of concreteness and plasticity. It is the response to human carnality.

May 31, 1984

The weakness that we feel when we agree to abandon everything that goes along with the Reality we have encountered, because this may be pure and unique, and the weakness that derives from the proposal to live the day in an orderly way—and for this reason always in the same way—are surmountable if we consider that they have to do not with a series of principles but with persons. They do not have to do with seeking to adjust our own acts as much as possible to an ideal model, but with deepening a friendship, a covenant. It is something vital, engaging, that makes the tension possible.

June 19, 1984

Horror vacui [12] afflicts us. To give oneself a goal to reach from time to time fills the day. But is this an authentic existence? There is, without a doubt, a wider sphere. We want to see these small ends framed in a larger context, characterized by the ideal principle. We want to reconnect the multiplicity of experiences in the unity of a meaning. With the passing of time, the small ends are felt as less demanding, less fascinating, and here the *horror vacui* enters in. At this point, we need the bigger principle: to give meaning to all the moments of the day, to live them as unrepeatable. Life is like a day, short. The ultimate end must be always present, alongside the small ends that we must fulfill during the week. This builds personal **history** (as opposed to a life without sense).

June 20, 1984

"The soul suspended in a new wonder, gliding over woods with outstretched arms, the flight of a seagull," [13] the sun that sets, the indefinite surge of emotion, Being that is so Being as to seem to us, cursed pessimists that we are, empty, Nothing. The new dimension, the new man. We have said **no** to all this. We have told ourselves no, said no to our life. When we didn't step beyond, when we settled, when we said that it was too difficult for us, too high. We have repeated the **no** to **life** when we have refused the **law** that refreshes the soul, that makes the simple wise, that makes the heart rejoice, that

---

12. Fear of empty space.
13. Lucio Battisti, *Slow Motion*, 1982.

gives light to the eyes (cf. *Psalm* 119:8–9). We need to have within ourselves the **chaos** to give birth to a dancing **star** (Nietzsche).

June 20, 1984

We find ourselves distracted. We have two possibilities: to put ourselves again on the highway or to let someone else transport us. From this **yes** or **no** we reach the decisive response. Starting from this moment, we build up or we tear down. We cannot preserve ourselves. Not even the palace, after it has been built, preserves itself. It gets old, it deteriorates. In the same way, we, at every moment, either grow or go backward.

June 22, 1984

The true pain, the one that breaks us down, is the sense of lack. Purgatory and hell are the lack of God. Now we suffer because we do not see directly. Yet we all have the possibility for joy because traces of the divine surround us in life. But the absolute lack (sin) will be truly tragic.

June 24, 1984

The passionate nature is attached to our own personal project, and to a smaller desire than that which is offered. Our equilibrium diminishes when, even if rationally conceiving the Ideal as the greater reality, in practice the desire to reach a partial objective dominates our life. This tension generates anxiety. The Christian vision does not oppose itself to this type of tendency, only frames it at a more breathable level. To be possessed by the Ideal should be a source of continual and stable joy, and this is the struggle that we must fight. Help comes from meditation, philosophically conducted, on the source of all the emotions and the good passions and happinesses. These aspirations, linked to something particular, will not be nullified, but fulfilled in the realm of hope that sustains us.

Joyful Days Ahead

June 25, 1984

Secularization is a phenomenon that touches us very closely, that has entered within us. It is manifested above all in the lack of sensitivity to the Principle that is the Answer to every human question and need. When we seek the answer through a personal project and not through a total surrender, we think implicitly that the Answer is only for some problems, and not for everyone.

July 1, 1984

There are two ways to resolve conflicts, enigmas, intricate situations, questions. The first is human and it is what fits more easily. It is instinctive. In front of a problem, we look for personal answers. The second way is the overcoming of instinct. It consists in becoming aware that there exists, on this earth, a living reality that enters in and conditions our history. The second way does not lead, though, to quietism,[14] but to rationality. Behind these two terms there are two different lifestyles: quietism and disengaged abandonment vs. rationality and the commitment that is the fruit of considerations that are often cancelled, forgotten, through human weakness. To clarify what kind of question we are referring to, we can give the examples of the choice of a future job and of matrimony. It is absurd to affirm that Someone we call Father does not have to do with these important matters. Or better, He might be absent from them, but only because of our rejection of Him.

July 5, 1984

The Christian choice is motivated by the Principle that has already manifested itself as a reality capable of changing existence.

---

14. Quietism was a 17th-century Catholic spiritual heresy that taught a distorted form of interior prayer and passivity.
It was formally condemned by Pope Innocent XI in 1687. The soul should stop making acts of will, desire, or effort.
One should remain in a state of complete stillness ("quiet") before God.

July 6, 1984

The expectation of something, the hope that it will happen, leads to an optimism that, sometimes, is without foundation, unrealistic. This happens when we are strongly conditioned by passions.

July 12, 1984

As in our studies, the intellectual progress we have made must push us to continue, despite the difficulties, the distractions, the tiredness. In the same way, in the religious realm, consideration of the difficulties should be joined to the meditation on the Reality that we have encountered and have intuited as the answer.

July 19, 1984

Maybe we have been told *do not judge* because many of those we have judged to be damaged in reality have found or will find salvation? The *do not judge* can be understood like this: *Be careful not to make false considerations about the possibility of someone's salvation. Many more than we think will be redeemed.*

July 21, 1984

Our *self* is outside of us; it seems ungraspable.

July 23, 1984

We can say with absolute certainty that the theme of renunciation occupies, in Christianity, a secondary place and, in the very end, an inconsistent place, for two reasons: 1) We speak of renunciation only in the sense that man should make the effort to regulate his senses, in order to be better on this earth. For this reason, the one who renounces his life will find it. 2) The last word of Christianity is **life**, the renunciation of renunciation. Immoderate passion is, instead, true renunciation, consistent renunciation, that leaves a mark.

July 23, 1984

If a renewed commitment to the Reality that has liberated us from anxieties and difficulties on the one hand requires a new effort, a new act of faith, on the other hand it is already a guarantee of success, of liberation. The fact of liberation that derives from the act of faith is a confirmation of the existence of an Intelligence that not only moves things, but also makes them harmonious.

July 23, 1984

The distribution of the trials through which we must pass, a distribution that adapts itself to the strengths that each person has, such that we cannot be tempted by a temptation stronger than our own strength, is the proof of the existence of an Operative Principle that is not far from man.

August 2, 1984

For you who rightly care about your honor, and want to avoid ridiculous attitudes, unusual words, tones that would end up limiting you, seek the Kingdom. This will make you assume the right attitudes, the true attitudes, except for necessary, but not substantial, adjustments.

August 6, 1984

We do not say that we have the Truth, because that would be false. Neither do we say that we feel ourselves always possessed by the Truth. Rather, we affirm that, day after day, we need to dust off reality in us, to remember. We need to remember that there is a Person who guides us in our way and who calls us to live life with a new enthusiasm, in whatever place and whatever circumstance we find ourselves. And we never find ourselves by chance in that place or that circumstance. We need every day to remember that this Presence has already changed our life, has already raised us up many times from anguish. Therefore, we never despair, but, animated by the hope for the future, seek to bring something perennial into the present.

August 17, 1984

Before judging a person, giving her advice, guiding her, we must feel again what she is experiencing. For example, in the case of existential nausea, we advise the other much better when we first relive those sensations. We thus remember the oppression, the sense of tightness and the path to take, to follow—the most difficult, truly the most difficult.

August 20, 1984

It seems like the more one feels bad on this earth, the more one desires to remain in that state. The more one is good, because he has found a certain equilibrium, the more he desires another life. To be good on this earth is to taste already the new heavens and the new earth. Obviously, if just a small taste is liberating, we will ardently desire its fulfillment. Outside of this, we fumble around in the darkness.

August 29, 1984

The attitude that makes our existence less authentic is loving more what is simply possible than what is real, present. Our attention is often more concentrated on what could be, on what we desire, rather than on what we possess. The object of desire, moreover, is colored to such an extent that it is presented to us as something decisive. When it becomes reality, it dissolves in our hands and is reduced to what it truly is. Since we find ourselves in one place instead of another, with some people and not others, with particular questions and commitments to face and not others, and all this not by chance, it is right to say with Nietzsche: "So I wanted it to be." But this time we say it with truth. The repetition of this phrase is the acceptance of a task that has been assigned to us.

September 7, 1984

Hope is the awareness of having within ourselves that Presence which is the Answer to all our problems.

Happiness is the consciousness, acquired experientially, that this Presence is truly the Answer to our problems. The level of happiness of a person is proportionate to the awareness of the Presence in him of Jesus Christ, He who frees us and renews us with a new enthusiasm.

Peace is the feeling of liberation that consists in recognizing that we are possessed and guided by a Reality greater than the miserable reality that we possess and in recognizing that the strength of this Reality is stronger than the strength of any passion, of any woman, of any melancholy, of any death. It is the perception of a unity, so alive as to annul the dispersive images that space offers us and time takes from us.

September 11, 1984

To be directed, strongly conditioned by a personal project, to love the realization of this project and to consume our energy in the attempt to bring it about, means to fall in love with that which cannot be loved without worry. The principle to follow is instead another. We must have one sole objective: the building of the Kingdom. This attitude frees us. It provokes a decentralization that leads to peace. Was it not maybe for this reason that it was said, "You have to lose your life if you want to save it" (*Matthew* 16:24–25)?

October 3, 1984

The non-Christian cannot hope to have in the future more than he has now. The Christian hopes with certainty to have in the future more than he now possesses. It is true that the non-Christian walks in the shadows, does not know where he goes. Effectively, outside of his projects of earthly success, in the end, he does not know where he is going.

November 13, 1984

To live keeping in mind the precarious situation in which we are, prevents profound delusions. Everything on this earth is contingent, everything is relative because everything is History. But even History gives way to the New, the Absolute.

December 11, 1984

What does it mean to *make straight the paths* except to prepare the soul for the arrival of the Lord?! The preparation of the soul, expectation, is not an action or an attitude that makes us the center of attention. What must be at work is an attempt of decentering, the abandonment of sentimentality, the acquisition of silence that leaves space to Him who comes. Silence of soul is the absence of worry about exams or of pride (only one thing is necessary: the Kingdom). It is the distance from emotions (which can sometimes be neurotic). Advent is the expectation of a Newness that we still do not know and that—thus it should be—will surprise us in the measure that we silence our useless thoughts about the past and the future.

December 30, 1984

The fixed idea that I have in mind in this period is that of overcoming my ego. It is true that the anguish of man consists in being tenaciously attached to something, to oneself, that is not the source of happiness. Happiness does not come from oneself but from something that is outside us. It seems to me that the vast majority of human suffering comes from the attachment to our ego. After all, it was not said in vain that the last defect to disappear is love of self. In short, in order to live authentically, we need to conquer the self; we need to lose ourselves in order to find ourselves. The best way and the most tangible way to lose ourselves is to entrust ourselves to a companionship.

January 1985

We need to try to fill with meaning even those few hours not determined by the community or by work, because with summer coming, which will present us with longer days and more time at our disposal, we know how to propose joyful moments, in a creative way, that reveal a redeemed atmosphere. The problems and the proposals are born from the difficulty of living time actively. Either we are creators in first person or we are subjected to weariness and nihilism.

January 20, 1985

In the measure by which we form our self-awareness by an attention to our person, our *passive sensitivity* grows. This kind of passivity is liberating because we are aware of something Other than the self. We need to forget ourselves to be at peace. We need to lose ourselves in order to find ourselves, to exercise our sense of belonging.

March 15, 1985

I thank the Lord for the openness to the world that he has given me, the overcoming of anguish, of a suffocation in which I was hermetically sealed. Openness to the world means for me a greater security in every field, to begin from human relationships in order to end in study and sport. I have received this gift through Communion and Liberation, which is everything for me because for me the Lord is everything. What other experiences are there that give a Christian education with these results, that give such a clean hit to individualism?

April 12, 1985

Openness to the world, testimony, an outgoing attitude, which a lived Christianity proposes, make us overcome theological positions that are too conservative and makes us open to the recognition of how much positivity there is in the *other*. Life influences the ideas we have.

April 23, 1985

We need to substitute one thing for the usual attitude, which consists in entrusting everything to our own capacities, for the anxiety over our projects, for the preoccupation of doing everything well and of determining the best attitude for others: the recognition of a powerful reality that waits only to be invoked in order to manifest the marvels of which it is capable. This *waiting* must become something structural, constitutive of the mind.

June 29, 1985

Boredom cannot exist for the Christian, because in every instant of his day something important is at play. When we find ourselves in particular situations where we cannot do what we like, when we find ourselves in circumstances that we have not chosen but in which we must remain—carrying out, for example, family duties—even then we are called to seek out the *authentic attitude* of that moment. Even when one doesn't do anything, when he has no obligation, when he is not called to anything, at least the gift of his time is at play.

September 12, 1985

The martyr is the one who has fully realized himself, the one who has more affection for himself than any other, the one who loves the *truth about himself* to the point of death. There is, therefore, one attachment to self that we call egoism and another that we call affection.

September 14, 1985

Our gestures are often not motivated by the Ideal but by the will to appear *in line* before others, or to surpass others, or to build, by ourselves, a community. But when will we start living a gesture connected solely to the Meaning?

September 24, 1985

Do I care for reality and use it in the most perfect, most intense, most adequate way with respect to my ultimate needs? Or do I, in a systematic way, not consider these ultimate needs for truth, for beauty, for justice that are the structure of my person, in order to give way to an instinctive search for goods that are more proximate, but at the same time more inconsistent?

September 25, 1985

When we speak about separating, dividing, not letting ourselves be invested by the Christian event, we must consider, for example, those periods of study when we think only about the exam, and say, *I will begin again later*. Instead, every instant should be lived within this new dimension. This is the way to know *that which is greater than our imagination*.

— We need to learn to esteem ourselves as persons, as subjects who have appeared mysteriously on this earth at a certain point in time. To esteem ourselves for what we are. To love the gaze with which we remain surprised, the unsettling gaze that arrived when we were not aware of ourselves, that revealed another dimension, opened another door. To desire, in light of this human gaze, the gaze of an Other. To want to be looked upon.

October 7, 1985

But what strikes us if not a gaze on ourselves that is totally "other"? It is a different gaze because it unsettles you, because it reveals something that is beyond your habitual categories of reason and feeling. It is the strangeness that is filled with positivity that gives itself unexpectedly, without calculation or strategy, gratuitously. It takes you to a deeper level of reason, of the heart. It takes all your heart. The second extraordinary thing is that this totally Other is *for* you.

October 7, 1985

Among human feelings or, rather, among the experiences that we live, the experience of falling in love is the most similar to the relationship with the Divine. The value of marriage is in this: it is made up of feelings and gestures analogous to those that characterize the religious life. It is a sign of a greater reality. For man, marriage is a way to practice ascesis toward God in so far as, through it, one is inserted, almost from the first, into a dimension that is ontologically different and that opens up new perspectives, connected to the sacred and to the sign.

Naples, October 29, 1985

Our greatness does not depend on the capacities that we have. At first we thought we were already intelligent, then the deception of this belief was revealed; we realized that we communicate little and that, in short, many others are better, are humanly more advanced. But on what does our greatness depend? On the capacities we can list? If it was this way, Christianity would be an occasion of competition just like everything else in this world. Instead, our greatness is in this: I did not exist and Someone wanted me on this earth; I was lost, without a life, and Someone saved me. Our greatness is in the fact that One loves you and this One is Everything.

November 27, 1985

The content of the Christmas poster corresponds to what happened to me in these last months, in particular where it says, "What lifts up and nourishes the awareness of self is the experience of a relationship in which the person is entirely recognized and welcomed" (beyond all his limits). The difficulties from which I am emerging, both quickly and unexpectedly (because one is always growing, but the speed is unexpected), are the doing of things out of duty, feeling moralistically responsible in front of the truth I have encountered. Moralism is something very narrow compared to the aspiration to be oneself. I am in the Movement now for this. One can be in the Movement only verbally when one does not see what it has to do with life. But why do I study? I start from anxiety in order to find an answer to it. Anxiety is a stimulus to re-center on the point. The point is the person, in personal relationship with the content of the companionship. The horizon is marked by the companionship, by the companionship understood as the horizon of a present event.

November 28, 1985

The environment in which we are moving is the one that is most concrete and most re-capitulatory of the question of life: the personal attitude in front of things. It always happens, in fact, that we have to assume an attitude in front of the circumstances, even those that seem the most banal. We cannot flee from this task. In case we would want to flee from this, we would not be bypassing the problem. It would only be resolved in a negative sense. Things pass over our head without being taken seriously. They happen without our involvement. We are neutral in front of them. Whether they exist or not, for us it is the same. The indistinct flux of time would decide our life; nothing stimulates us, nothing involves our human position. Something different can happen, when the circumstances provoke our life emotionally or maybe even rationally, whether positively or negatively. *A thought that does not come to fruition* is enough to break down our life. We endure the circumstances or, in the best cases, these circumstances provoke happiness (unstable like everything else, because everything passes away). There is a third possibility: it is characterized by an attentive gaze on things and at the same time by the *possession* of a criterion of judgment on reality that does not define the outcome of our actions or of the circumstances of life as absolutely decisive. There is something greater than things, as a possibility to remember that *criterion of judgment*. We see everything as a possibility for human growth (we can speak about human growth only when we know where to put the bricks for building). We face everything with greater surrender, because everything is good. Everything can be taken from us, but not the positivity that we have encountered. We put ourselves in play in the circumstances starting from this criterion. Everything is good even if it goes badly. The positive is beyond the vacillating results. Everything becomes a good or the hope for a good.

In a definitive way, every gesture is either to build or to destroy. In order to build we need to be motivated not by the contingencies that emerge from the circumstances but from the criterion we have mentioned. This criterion is the memory of the Event, rationally awakened regardless of the emotional effect that can be produced or not. Only in this case are we not slaves of the situation.

We ordinarily live by seeking the realization of something of ours (girls, exams, etc.). We depend on something. We need a goal and if it does not come about, we crumble. And if it does come about, we crumble all the same. There is something that allows us to take life in our hands, that makes us stronger. Culture is a familiarity with this Factor, which is a criterion that always makes us grow, in any circumstance, that does not make us just endure things.

Immediately, the gestures are an obstacle, but if we do not pass through these difficulties, we do not grow. The effort is not an obstacle; it is the condition for growth. The drama comes when you are struck by something—everything is for this.

Has the beginning of that passage to personal awareness within the circumstance happened? Within the contingency that I live, I must love more what I have encountered. If it does not happen like this, we are not an example. Life tends to come down to this. What is the step that we must take? An attitude impedes us from learning in front of large or small things. We reduce the great desire that we have to a particular fact. We cannot circumscribe the desire that we have (to circumscribe some feeling or other, this does not make us face everything in life). It has to do with living reality within this awareness in order not to be afraid in front of what happens. What happens is a possibility, it is renewed within the circumstances. It is the only business of life. Christmas places us again within reality with this awareness. The feasts are an occasion because, starting from what one has lived, the event shows itself. Christmas is not a recognition but a welcoming, to have a connection with this Event. When we are restricted in a particular, we must return to the origins. How come this desire does not always renew itself, and a particular prevails in the circumstances? When we do not connect it to a recognition that has happened in our life. What you live corresponds more to you—this is the source of a change of attitude. There is something that comes just before us, that loves us.

The day is full of anxieties, fears, and timidity. This time is for re-centering our attention on what transforms difficulties into possibilities. When we face something that we do not like, we always ask if this is the ultimate thing that we encounter or if something greater exists. My desire for these days is to re-center the question. To what do I belong?

Our inadequacy in front of reality hurts. It is possible to recover if we make the effort to re-center ourselves around Christ, the exhaustive meaning of everything. Here is the struggle of life. The desire for fulfillment. It is not connected to introspection or to an emotional transport or to a duty. The practicality of desire is connected to reality in the complexity of its call (requests or duties). We do everything in the hope that, in facing things, there will appear in these, sooner or later, the content of our experience, that is not friendship with another, who is limited like us, but One capable of giving fulfillment to your destiny. What is the reason for accepting the effort? The hope that Christ will show Himself in the circumstance.

December 21, 1985

It is taken for granted that we will fall. What is not taken for granted is that we will get up again, because this has a condition that not everyone accepts, and that is humility. It is the poverty of recognizing that there is One who is greater than the image you have in your head. Alone you cannot raise yourself up. You have to accept your weakness and entrust yourself to an Other. We prefer our own measure, which consists in believing no morality or order is possible, rather than to adhere to a measure that is not ours, to the way things go.

February 14, 1986

"I will see the goodness of the Lord in the land of the living" (*Psalm* 27:13). Whatever positivity there is in life is part of the goodness of the Lord. There is nothing to hope for in life outside of this. Hope is the expectation of a good ending, that which raises us up.

February 16, 1986

It sometimes happens that we distinguish moments we deem appropriate from moments that are not opportune to live this tension. We set aside certain times of the day, and then—we say—there will come a better time to pose the question of our attitude in front of our lives. In this way, certain aspects of life are censured, and we believe they are *neutral* situations. We wait for them to pass. This is not how it is, though, because every situation, every state of soul is not so by chance. They are rather places to work; those situations, if they pass unobserved, pass by forever. They are unrepeatable, unique, as are the outcomes they hide, the perspectives that they open. From what can we start again if not from the exact horizon in which we find ourselves immersed? The horizon is the existential situation where we are in a definite moment. It is the sum of external and internal factors which in that precise moment define the person.

February 16, 1986

In this phase, characterized by a tension that continually rises up, I risk falling into the aridity of continual, mechanical repetition: the effort to remember. What saves me from the aridity is the memory of the initial gaze that allowed me to walk so quickly. This memory of people—and not of mechanisms—gives life a new pulse.

February 28, 1986

My desire now is to see the activities of the day beat to the rhythm of a time that is perceived differently. I no longer see a scattering of images, but something that gathers the multiplicity into one; a new rigor, under the Shadow of one who never goes away.

March 4, 1986
Belonging
Belonging is first of all the recognition of an ontological bond with one's own origin. Existentially, this ontological link translates into spending time with a companionship and into a profession of faith. Definitively, though, it is the recognition of a mercy that works on you, of a surprising gaze that touches the root of the self.

March 4, 1986
An all-embracing beauty
It is true that there is both a general and a particular memory. It is also true that the latter, applied to various facets of life, requires a realistic commitment. It is even more true that there exists a level that is reduced to a point in the human soul: once this is shaken, everything is shaken and every facet of life is affected. There is a root that is difficult to reach, and even more difficult to wrap your mind around. Moreover, it is impossible for the human will to shake it off. We can only work on it. But we grasp the root intuitively, and this produces results that human strength, anxious and dispersed in the multiplicity of factors, cannot even hope to produce. This happens when one falls in love, which is a sign, among the clearest signs, that man needs an all-embracing beauty. This all-embracing beauty makes you understand that you are in the hands of the Lord, in the strong sense. When He wants, you are shaken. And all your efforts, in this perspective, seem a little thing (but they are not).

Two Lenten concerns

I have two current concerns. The first is the rediscovery of the self, because we have misplaced it. It is lost. We want to find it again. It is distant from us. Our heart is arid, compressed, flattened, lifeless. We have lost it because we have pursued the realization of a scheme, rather than our true face. We have lost ourselves in this. The other concern is the present awareness of belonging, understood as awareness of a Gaze or of *the protective Shadow (Psalm*

121:5). A spark is missing: that the heart be touched, in its roots, by a renewed Gaze, so that the heart can open up.

March 20, 1986

My hope is to deepen the relationship with the reality that I have encountered, because it is the only thing that has corresponded to me. People have welcomed me. There is in me the certainty that the more I become familiar with the content of this companionship, the more there grows in me the strength to face everything. This desire of being stronger, of turning things around in my life, of overcoming my baseless fears, has made me assume a different attitude in front of things and has made me accept the continued effort. This hope for change, in fact, is, for me, tied to a work and to an active position in front of the circumstances that I live. For example, in front of the meaningful relationships that I have, I realize that my hope, my desire for change, is alive when I seek to draw the best out of these relationships, when I commit myself. It often happens, though, that the lack of vigilance makes me lose many opportunities. How do we become more vigilant?

May 1, 1986

Together with a degree of awareness that I have never reached before now, I notice the urging of a subtle choice between study, which is connected to my dreams of human success, or Christianity. The choice is subtle because study is at the same time an instrument of power and an instrument of love for the Fact. *I should study more.* This is an affirmation that I can repeat in a Christian way or in a vain way. The desire to study more generates anxiety because there is not enough time in the day. Anxiety is the sign of a mistaken position. I lack faith, a faith understood as trust (think about the Kingdom, the rest will be given you in abundance).

May 2, 1986

Prayer is the memory of Christ, which conquers again the unity lost to our dispersion in multiplicity. Prayer makes present what is Other than the self, which means *different* with respect to what we think, what we believe, what we hope. The person continues to fall into idolatry, so much so that life is a drama until the end. That is, it is a struggle between our own measure and a measure that is not ours. The drama always repeats itself and life is a continual temptation, because the overcoming of a partial scheme, a form of idolatry, does not make us reach the finish line. A partial horizon, while it is a point of arrival, is, a second later, a new point of departure to make a new choice. Prayer lashes us because it presents the Other to man's heart. It drives us where we do not want to go, to belong to the Reality we have encountered, which, compared to the evil project or the best proposal, cannot be grasped beforehand. It is a jump into the dark, an adherence to what exists but which we do not know, a risk that we always accept anew. But on closer inspection, that apparent absence of everything, that darkness without shape, that we must embrace, is the place of life, *the land flowing with milk and honey*, which we reach only when we have a companionship.

Nihilism

We are inevitably plunged to the bottom of this age of nihilism. We carry on our shoulders the weight of solitude in front of destiny, the absence of a Meaning in everyday life. It is impossible these days to be tranquil.

Against moralism

We must always seek out an active solution. Moralism first makes us recognize the weight of a situation, then makes us choos—in the sense of renunciation. Realistically, though, renunciation is legitimate only when viewed from the perspective of something greater. What gives us pleasure often seems excessive, and we bring out non-existent problems. We are on the way only when we recognize a positive attitude in ourselves.

The companionship

There is a fundamental point in man where he receives and is given companionship. It can only be reached and seen by the eyes of the mind. It is beyond the psyche; it is called the heart. *Genesis*, in the story of the creation of the woman, tells us this. In daily life, the task is to search for unity, for companionship among men, considering the other according to his heart.

Morality: the beautiful and the true

A practical criterion for judging the morality of a gesture and of an action consists in measuring the beauty of it. The beautiful is measured, harmonic, without displacements, proportioned, adequate. Human action, in so far as it is not beautiful, is not morally good. Examples of this concept can be found in the area of human affection, where our instincts often prevail. This is not adequate to the fundamental expectations of the other person, or the tenderness that is due to the other. Or we can consider the organization of evenings with friends, songs, jokes, words, and the like. The theoretical justification of this principle is in the fact that, ontologically, truth is connected to beauty inasmuch as the latter reveals and manifests the former.

Morality: codification and dynamism

Even today, a certain theology and a certain philosophy attempt to encompass reality within a few perennial schemes. They are characterized by the forgetfulness of what's real and by thinking according to immutable categories. This way of posing morality has led to that scrupulosity of conscience among people that twists the meaning of Christianity into a Christianity that is no longer an encounter that opens to all the aspects of reality, but a religion of precepts that aims to distinguish evil things from good things. More particularly, all that is joy, life, pleasure, is either evil in itself or is a momentary concession made to man. Traditionalism is characterized by a rigid observation of what has been sanctioned in the past and by the absence of a living encounter in the present. The moral conception that comes out of this is obviously that of the precept, something analytical; it tends to exclude the categories of gradualness and historicity. In Christianity understood as a living and present Fact, the encounter comes first and then morality. The concreteness of living comes first and then the law that is a guide to understanding reality. Otherwise it is a noose around the neck.

July 1986

Impatience

The principle of every human action is founded on the observation of reality in motion and on the assumption of a position or of an adequate attitude that we reach through a return to the self and an eventual revision. In this context, impatience leads to the triumph of psychological reactions disengaged from reality. These produce an anxiety that would try to hurry up the time with which reality moves itself. The overcoming of impatience, which is a way man distances himself from reality, needs an energy that connects us to reality. This energy is a pure grace; we can simply request it in an open and dynamic way.

Returning to the things themselves

We escape from the circle of vain intellectualism only within an encounter that reawakens us. When we ask about the meaning of life, we sometimes risk not reaching the level of *things themselves*. Something schematic is still present. There is a wall to get over. The question about meaning is not an idea, but something that occurs before the action happens and within a horizon of memory—that is, an enveloping stream that starts from the existence of a companionship. Only when the question occurs in front of a fact that we do not understand do we begin to live at the level of the things themselves. However, there is a strict connection between the Meaning of things and reality. The origin of the person and of reality is the same. Only if the subject recovers meaning can he recover all of reality.

Meaning—Subject—Reality

The subject that returns to the Meaning does not conquer the multiplicity of things, but their fundamental point. In this sense, the soul is in some way everything. The subject that enters into relationship with the ultimate meaning of things recovers also and above all his own original image. ("Made in the image and likeness of God.") He finds in front of himself the true image already realized, which is what he had lost.

Beyond the obvious

The *beyond* that makes life dynamic is to be understood in two fundamental directions. On the one side, it has to do with going beyond the schemes that suffocate vitality, in a rediscovery of reality as an event, of being an intensive act. On the other side, the beyond must be understood in the sense of a presentiment, that is, man should dispose himself in an attitude of asking, of ultimate openness beyond the negative circumstances that bring with them the temptation to nihilism. There are marginal experiences that are contradictory in themselves; by themselves, they cannot be explained. In these moments, we should note the need for the beyond. The Truth is an event.

July 23, 1986 (Vacation in Folgarida)

I looked at this trip, with all the newness that it brought, a reality so strange, something so new in itself, almost without fear. When fears did appear, they were conquered. The criterion to face these circumstances has been the criterion of faith. Faith conquers everything. For the vacation, my desire is to recover this criterion. In fact, the criterion of elementary experience is something we must always conquer again and again. Reality, because of the character that I have, can be faced head on only if in the present I move myself beginning from that criterion. It is difficult to have to admit to ourselves that we need people to conserve and cultivate a vigilance on ourselves. This admission happens at the level of personal movement.

When we find ourselves again in front of an objectivity (people and realities) that in an evident way go beyond the habitual horizon within which we normally live, there is a renewed desire to go beyond. We recognize that we still have grown so little. This vacation has led me to the discovery of the complexity of reality and has clarified for me that this corresponds to me, that I need a reasonableness in facing things. My present desire is to break the stream of naturalness, of spontaneity, of just going with the flow, to burst into reality with decision, intention.

August 5, 1986

Reality must be conquered; we need to burst into reality and overcome the banks of the natural flow. The phrase "in the soothing softness of the modern world" (Alexis Carrel) means that we learn much more from a bike ride than from a trip in a car. In the first case, we dare, we challenge reality, we seek. In the second, we don't. Each particular contains everything. Even a bike ride can make the laws of life shine forth.

August 6, 1986

Beyond the feeling, there is the possibility of turning to a technique that is always applicable. This technique goes beyond instinct and, before everything, must be learned. For example, the technique of prayer is marked by pauses, by tone, etc. Only starting from technique can we reawaken a strong feeling.

August 7, 1986

A day is saved when, hour after hour, we decide again to avoid dispersion, when, hour after hour, insurmountable barriers are placed up.

January 5, 1987

Fraternity

To remain month after month at the same level of awareness is, at the very least, a waste of time. We must, without impatience, go forward. It is enough to begin by paying attention to things for only five minutes in the course of the day. It is enough to begin by living for five minutes in the dimension of memory. This is the dimension of attention without exaggerations, of vigilance without force, of a dynamic tranquility. It is the horizon in which the person is present to himself and understands things more deeply, understands the unity with another person, the richness of the companionship that does not fade away. Even the particular, which is most insignificant, as, for example, sitting next to someone you know, assumes a new face, is not obvious, is something worthy of reflection, something that spurs our thought. Our thought is spurred on when there is a true presentiment of reality (cf. Heidegger or Gadamer). The awareness that what is in front of you is still to be discovered, is greater than the mental categories you have. But the problem is not to have a true intuition of things. In order for the truth to touch the whole person, we must risk putting our person in play. This is the only way that the truth can impact the *sphere of life*. To put ourselves in play in a particular is to respect the concreteness of which man is made. A girl (romance) is a privileged point of comparison, the level at which we personally experience the event of existence—the greatest possibility of putting ourselves in play with the other; the crucible that allows us to overcome obstacles, passing through the sieve of our weaknesses, our moralism, and all the talents that we did not want to put in play because of fear. This experience recovers, in our own lives, the dimensions that have been set aside, those that have become rigid, become sterile because they were never shaken up. It is to go through the long way of recovering our physicality, which we always thought was base, which was not an object of life and therefore neither of reflection. It is a question of position. Either everything is obvious and worn-out, or everything is new, day after day. There are two elements that allow us to live an event as a new experience: 1) a presentiment, an affective tone that conceives of man as a planner and the world as possibility; 2) a rule that we read from time to time in reality, the fruit of our reflection on the situation that we are living. In other words, we must intuit the further step to take, to look forward to its execution, and carry it out. This second point helps us not to lose ourselves in abstract thought and to move within a history. The instruments for these things to happen are:

1) Prayer

2) Risk in a particular

The rediscovery of the companionship as the only place where change is possible.

The origin of our ordinary sufferings is not the lack of correspondence between the situation in which we find ourselves and what we would like instead, but in the lack, in the present, of the awareness that there is a horizon of meaning that is greater than the circumstances we are living. When we live within this lack, it is the situation that determines the state of soul, and not the meaning of things. From here comes suffering without end—that is, without meaning.

Anguish

Anguish is that emotional situation characterized by the recognition that things do not have a meaning. Why should we get up in the morning and repeat the same gestures we did the previous day? What prospect is there before our gaze? It seems like there is nothing. Are we going toward anything? When there is nothing stimulating before the eyes, in the day, there is nothing left to do but to grasp the present to oneself, painfully, the present moment, so as not to think about any future prospects, so as not to open oneself to the dimension of the future that does not offer anything. The contraction that happens in the present, which comes necessarily when we do not manage to live truly, is highly educative for the one who lives exclusively from nostalgia or from dreams without foundation. In any case, in the present, anguish reveals itself as the absolute absence of an outlook in the short term. Anguish goes forward only when there is a patient waiting for something to change and, even before that, because we recognize with our reason that there is a meaning in all this. It is like passing through a crucible. Anguish manifests itself when, even though all our dreams are realized, we are left empty handed, unable any longer to delude ourselves that reaching our goals is enough. Anguish touches the root of the person, for whom everything else no longer has an immediate significance; we recognize a meaning objectively, but that is not enough for us to feel better. Anguish renders us inactive in front of everything. We no longer manage to pray but when we do, prayer begins to be the only consolation and anguish tends to disappear. Anguish flourishes in the absence of a tradition. There is nothing outside, in the world, that is a stimulus or a refuge; everything is corrupted, not by a moralistic corruption, but by that corruption that comes from the withdrawal of the source of life.

Monday, February 9, 1987

In order to learn, we must take risks, and risk implies a daily dying to self.

February 21, 1987

The origin of pain: absence of realism
A large part of pain is provoked by our thoughts: situations in the future or the past, fears or regrets. Living the present moment is the way to recover a meaning.

February 24, 1987

The true companionship is not the companionship in which we share a work, but the one which makes us perceive a dimension of the heart corresponding to our true face. The companionship, if it is true, is a companionship in desiring, in questioning, in searching.

February 26, 1987

Pain in the present reveals the heart by enlarging it.

Joyful Days Ahead

History

"The aim of life is not to live but to die and to give your life joyfully" (Paul Claudel, *The Tidings Brought to Mary*). To die is the daily overcoming of a prejudice, of a presumption. In the measure that our presumption diminishes, the feeling of freedom grows. To want to die is possible only within a present awareness of the religious sense that abides in us. It is possible only within the awareness of our own finiteness. What remains, after death of prejudice and projects, is a will to give ourselves that generates joy. We live for a purpose. We look at the other differently. We learn from this to look differently at others, with an attention to their destiny. The only freedom that exists is the freedom of giving without any personal claims.

The danger of idolatry is always present. Our lack of respect for fashion actually shocks others. We understand better that for many the only real image is fashion. What is there other than a good outfit for a week in the mountains?

Campitello Matese, February 1987[15]

The foundation of our gift and our witness is in an offering of the self. It is not a discourse, but the physical offering of a day. It is a risk (which is never as great as we imagine it to be). There is a risk in embracing a new dimension, a role that does not fall within our standards. When we would like to do something else, we find ourselves instead on a hike in the snow with GS.

We must die daily; we must joyfully despise our life.

Freedom is possible only within a foolishness, the foolishness of taking lightly the *problems of life*, the systems in which we live, the problematic relationship.

---

15. This refers to a day in the mountains with the Student Youth (GS), just like the trip during which, exactly one year later, Giovanni died.

1) To establish a personal relationship with that **You** that is made present to you: to say in your room **You** , just like you say you to a friend or a girl. This is something literal.

2) The image of this **You** comes from the history you have lived, that you are living, not from prejudice.

3) Only this **You** gives you the strength to risk, that is, to do things that are foolish according to the common mentality: to break the bonds of an ordinary existence.

4) Freedom is the capacity to play, that is, to do things outside of the program. The program is the image that you have built of your day, the image in which you think you are at peace while in reality you are suffocating.

5) Power blames and pressures you and pushes you to complicate things; it takes that light innocence away from you.

School of Community

What prevailed in these days? The root of the religious sense or something else? The criterion of the School of Community or distraction? Reality, in these days, questions you, above all through *set moments*: the School of Community, studies, the elections. What are the reasons, beyond feeling, that move you within these solicitations? The dilemma is between the measure that reality dictates and your own imagination. The risk becomes clear in the acceptance of the criterion that opens you to reality; this acceptance is apparently foolishness, because you must joyfully despise your program. From here comes freedom from worries. The risk is not foolishness when it has reasons. The reasons, in the end, are synthesized in one word: Christ. The beginning and end of every action is Christ, to want to live a friendship with the only reality that is fully for you, that does not say *further on* (Montale).

1) School of Community—sentimentalism and study. Has someone said that our work here is at an end? It is here that the work properly begins.

2) Following—to adhere to reality in its concreteness: the companionship.
3) Prayer—to say **You**.

11 March 11, 1987

Absence of Authority

1) Disconnected thoughts, boredom, states of weariness: we do not have what we want. But the problem is something else.
2) The loss of the sense of sin.
3) "How sweet your words are to my taste" (*Psalm* 119:103). The dialectic: there is no sweetness without bitterness.

   A) Every perspective has its risk. *Eudaimonism*, that is, a conception of the faith that starts from the desire for happiness that is in man, can generate a claim to an immediate response, conceived according to subjective criteria. The times and the modes of *happiness* are then dictated by me. From here, in its turn, comes faith in an object built by man. We only accept the response to our question/need through the outlines that our fantasy has traced. This also applies to the field of knowledge, of thought, existentially, as a state of soul. The claim prevails that reality should conform to our anxiety for fulfillment. This way of proceeding leads to anguish, that is, to the lack of meaning (of an answer). The lack of **authority** is real because Western culture has gradually moved its attention from objective being to the subject (conceived in a narcissistic way as distant from the world). The first point is no longer the objective law but the pretentious claims of the subject. No longer does man bend himself to the authority that imposes itself, but reality must bend itself to the caprice of the subject. In the measure that authority is absent, man oscillates and wanders in a disconnected way. In the absence of authority, a certain *morning psychologism*[16] finds space—that is, the piling up of anguished thoughts as well as boredom and states of weariness. The freedom of man who is disconnected from the Center is a freedom gone crazy. Either we take refuge in a partial goal or in the claim to be god, which however does not answer our need. It is also true that the claim to be god arises in the absence or in the forgetfulness of being,[17] and that, moreover, the sensible event of an authority in our life is a grace. It is not even enough to say *authority exists*; we need a subject that is constitutionally disposed to recognize authority.

B) The absence of this predisposition, which is not structural, but acquired in time, regards the subjective dimension and is manifest in the *loss of the sense of sin*. All that is left is a moralistic concept of sin, which expresses itself either in scrupulosity or laxity, which are two positions that are formally diverse but substantially traceable to the same root. The loss of the sense of sin ends up in a schism between faith and life, in the gradual passage from a global to a devotional faith. Conceiving of God as a term of one's own consciousness, depending on the situation, dissolves itself in nothing (because a subjective idea, sooner or later, fades away). Even when a tenuous link with objective reality is conserved, we understand God as a punishing judge of subjective actions deprived of any global value.

The horizon of faith gets restricted: from a horizon that excludes nothing, we move to a narcissistic, egocentric horizon. How else can we explain, for example, that the scrupulous are attentive in the use of their language and completely superficial in the things that really matter? In this point of view, scrupulosity

---

16. When there is a lack of external direction or purpose, thoughts become overwhelming or negative.

17. Forgetfulness of being refers to the essential nature of our existence.

is joined to a concept of Authority that tends to narrow life, to set aside certain aspects of it (from here comes the sense of inferiority of Christians). Authority, in short, has lost its original fascination, which was founded on the fact that it moved us to open ourselves to a perspective bigger than the bourgeois perspective.

March 21, 1987

The distance of the person from himself shows up in the fact that we do not do many things, we do not risk much, we do not enter into action. We remain at the window, either in moralism, or in our comfort zone. This distance from the self means that life is lost. To recover ourselves, we need to reconquer life. The only way to reconquer life is to begin to practice it. Until now, faith was strong because it was applied to a narrow reality. The risk, the bet, begins now, because faith must face the reality we encounter, something much more vast. There is in this risk the fascination of becoming experts of life, of overcoming the state of dependency. The time for a cautious defense of our talents is over. The promise is the overcoming of moralism, the broadening of horizons, the overcoming of inferiority complexes, the power to bring our faith, by affirming it, to a higher level, a level that is more astute, more experienced. A faith that is *pure* is at an end; now we must create faith again by entering into life.

March 23, 1987

— *Caritas* as a presentiment (which dictates an attitude in front of reality). To fix ourselves on this.

— *Caritas* above *eros* and *philia*.

— Two alternative positions: the will to power or succumbing in front of reality (fear).

— The sublimation of these two alternatives: to feel ourselves masters of the world ("all is yours")[18] or to accept objective reality. The two true needs, which give rise to distorted

---

18. Saint Paul, 1 *Corinthians* 3:22

positions, are met in charity (love, a true relationship with the given reality).

March 24, 1987

The great temptations in this period have to do first of all with the practical rejection of reality, which does not correspond to my thoughts and projects, and because of which I am neither studying nor preparing my lessons. Then, there is worry about the future. There is a response to each of these temptations: obligation, censure, love (which comes first). All within a rediscovery of **meaning**.

March 28, 1987

Tradition and Sensus Fidei

The Movement educates the *sensus fidei*.

The *sensus fidei* is a presentiment. Medieval philosophy, like the Bible, is known authentically only within a living tradition, which subjectively makes the *sensus fidei* come alive.

April 16, 1987

Spiritual Exercises: The signs are clear; the way has been marked out. Now is the time for responsibility.

April 18, 1987

The many circumstances of life, including those that cause embarrassment, exist to bring out an active position. The active position is what must be recovered continually and marks the strength of a person in front of reality and the different situations that arise. We are referring particularly to shyness.

May 18, 1987

Loneliness is increasing again. Loneliness is the absence of meaning.

May 20, 1987

There is a drama that is faced starting from intuition, presentiment. It has to do with the alternative between the activity of the soul and passivity. It is a presentiment, and therefore decides the way in which we confront any element of reality. It is a universal drama because it is always applicable; it is an *alternative-key*.

May 22, 1987

The evil to fight is introversion, with all that it generates: suspicion, jealousy, lack of trust, sadness, passivity, obsessive thoughts, scruples, excessive analysis, lack of elasticity, quibbling.

May 23, 1987

After making a mistake—we are referring to what was indicated above—there comes the anxiety to repair it. But it is clear that this is not possible, that reality is greater. The evidence remains that it is reasonable to entrust ourselves to one who has begun a relationship with and supports the rhythms of this relationship, with humility, without moralism or desire to possess. **No one belongs to you.**

May 25, 1987

There are joyful days ahead because I have asked the Lord to be able to serve Him.

May 26, 1987

God is jealous. Jealousy in its greatest degree is a feeling that does not tolerate that the other person may think or do something independently from the person that is jealous. Every gesture and every thought should have one end, one goal: to strengthen the unity with the other person, to be completely related to the other person. This allows God to possess us. What is unacceptable, in the extreme degree, between men is a duty in front of God.

May 27, 1987

Will to possess. We slip unknowingly into a will to possess, above all when there is no explicit opposition. Until now we have wanted to lead the other person into our own rhythms, our own ideas, without a respect for objective truth, which always calls us to a dispossession of self and of reality.

May 28, 1987

The multiplication of the loaves: The need is sacred in so far as it is a sign of the *question*.

May 29, 1987

Silence

Mother Teresa of Calcutta has proposed silence as the first step to reach beatitude and has indicated the following itinerary: silence, prayer, faith, charity. In the love of our neighbor we reach happiness and live in it. Happiness is given to a heart not turned in on itself but open to Otherness. In fact, memory is the awareness of self in so far as it is linked to the Christian companionship. The silence of speaking and hearing: we must return to silence to feel again the fundamental call of things, their primordial meaning. This has nothing to do with effort, but with disposing of ourselves to a gift. The clearest image is the sound of the drum in the silence of the virgin forest. The drum has meaning in silence. There is a dialectical relationship, inasmuch as the message exists with silence as its background, inasmuch as we don't hear anything else. Noise confuses the meaning, the message.

Adhering to Being

In the circumstances, we should give supremacy to Being, not to the awareness we have of ourselves, not to our own scheme. The circumstances have laws and we must adhere to these. We must immerse ourselves in study, forgetting everything else.

It is strange to hear Catholics sing: "The answer is blowing in the wind" (Bob Dylan). Either the song has some hidden or symbolic sense, or—more likely—we don't know what we are saying.

Memory as a vital stream

The principle of all true knowledge and of every action is in the interiority of man. This is the seat where our familiarity with destiny takes off and grows, little by little. This interiority is traditionally called Memory, but it is also indicated with other terms like *unity*, because man returns to himself and finds God who makes the truest part of the self, his essence, the root of his self, emerge. Another expression that we can use is *compunctio cordis*, which stresses the gathering of the cognitive and ethical energies in a single point of the soul, which the Bible calls *heart*. Memory is life in a vital stream, something objective, which man always has the possibility to touch, once it is gratuitously offered to him. The whisper of the Spirit, ever after, remains a gift, but it requires from man a struggle to win over, hour after hour, the point of origin. This work is called *ascesis* and is realized in the comparison of everything, starting from the *principle of the self*, with elementary experience. To throw ourselves again into this flow—this is the work. To face, head on, an objectivity that must be conquered anew—this is the law of life. Such a law, in fact, does not only have to do with the heart of man, but also with the energy that comes from this, that is, the energy of intelligence and freedom. These too must take hold of the objective stream that—in the beginning—is distributed in the various fields, the various disciplines. Through such energy, the possibility of achieving unity again is offered. For example, prayer is already the gentle belonging to something that goes by itself according to laws which man must obey. Moreover, we do not think our thoughts, but it is Thought that thinks in us. This topic of Idealism, if developed, would lead us to distinguish, on the one hand, the gradation of thoughts, from those studied by psychoanalysis (the obsessive thoughts that are not provoked by man, but which come from a strange region, one that is pathological) to those that, as *Psalm* 16 says, the night suggests ("Even at night my heart instructs me"—*Psalm* 16:7). On the other hand, we should distinguish what comes from the evil one and what instead is suggested benignly.

Gadamer wrote that the word speaks in us. Even here an objectivity returns, a foundation on which to draw. Gadamer, for this reason, anyway, is not able to develop his thought, to say that the foundation is the Word. In fact, if there is a foundation on which we can draw, it contradicts leaving space open to an absurd *without foundation*. The game, the festival, and the gathering enter into the same dynamic: to enter into their flow—which changes the rhythm of time in so far as it gives density, richness, and takes from it the weight of boredom and hard effort that never ends—we must overcome the barrier of laziness, of shyness, or of something else, depending on the situation. But this barrier can be overcome only if we start out from an original Meaning. Finally, the most important thing: The Event of Christianity is an historical fact, communicated 2,000 years ago, that is still alive. Christianity is an objective movement that guides those who adhere to it. The essence of Catholicism is given by this Presence, alive in history. It is like a wave that moves. It is not just a blowing in the wind, as in the cases mentioned, but *the* blowing of the Spirit *par excellence*. The challenge of life is to participate in this stream.

Recovering intelligence

We must study, not to finish the program, but to exercise intelligence and familiarize ourselves with its natural level, that which touches the essence of things. If a page of your book does not lead you to this level, it is a lost page. There is the level of the intelligence or else the level of imbecility (memorizing without understanding). We do not understand the page because we are in a rush. We want to finish the program, but we lose more time in this way.

Movement

Life plays itself out in this horizon: the movement as a living reality, *the* place (it is *the* place because it is not one among many, a place of engagement, of judgment. It is the living Church. It is among us in this moment) in which we find again the deepest content that corresponds to the question, the place where Christ is always present.

1) We need to recognize that there is nothing that is not filled by this.
2) Everything that we have is meant to nourish the Movement and make it grow.

Holiness

Imitation, an essential element in man's life, goes off track when it is just the mockery of vain images, according to fashion. It finds its common dimension in the family, its fulfillment and its apex in **holiness**. The Church is characterized also by a precise codification of human experience in general, in the sense that it shows this experience to us in its fulfillment. Nature and super-nature are not in contrast; they are on the same line even though at different levels.

What is the religious sense? 1)It is a series of questions on the meaning of life, on the consistency of reality, on the fragility and mystery of man's life. 2) Practically, it manifests itself in a search that is always renewed, because we always experience a new lack, an emptiness, a boredom. a) The experience of anguish and its difference from a particular painful event. b) The search for novelty, for the extraordinary, for the unusual (horror; hard rock and heavy metal; the Paris-Dakar rally).

— The level of these questions must always be reawakened. Otherwise, we live life unaware of ourselves; we do not know our own person. Today's world does not welcome this natural desire but guides it toward consumeristic forms to bring in more economic profits, or it exorcises it by reducing it or annulling it in a scheme of life deprived of excitement and emotion in the double temptation of conformism: fashion and systemization.

— Christianity is a way to reawaken desire, which makes us glimpse a complete answer, which is Christianity lived in its integrity.

— The method of observation goes beyond discussions on improbable, default metaphysical structures. The comprehension of phenomena goes beyond intellectualism, the breaking of the intellectual circle of words unfastened from reality. The **phenomenology** of contemporary life is the desire that dwells in man (*The NeverEnding Story*, *The Lord of the Rings*).

The most evident note that emerges from the film *The NeverEnding Story* is a search for newness that finds expression in the film in the Kingdom of Fantasia, a kingdom not connected to banality, to daily life considered as a grey absence of excitement. We must underline also the important aspect of the attack of *Nothing* that is silently destroying the foundation of Fantasia. The inhabitants cannot save themselves alone. They need a child who brings salvation, liberation. In films like *Rambo*, or in different songs, characters with a *deep look*, who are strong and mysterious, assume a place of importance. These characters never reveal all of themselves; they have zones of unreachable shadows. Their sunglasses hide an inscrutability, something that cannot be fully understood and therefore cannot be fully dominated. In the *Lord of the Rings*, a new horizon comes out, dense with symbols that refer to a meaning that both reveals and conceals at the same time. What do we deduce from all this?

1) Desire for novelty
2) Desire for mystery
3) Desire for meaning

Is Christianity an adequate response to this need for meaning? Is it something persuasive? Is it a newness or only something tiresome, obvious, childish? Christianity is the only true and authentic answer to the expectations of man. When it is not understood in this way, it is because we are closed to the other or because the Christian phenomenon is reduced to one of its aspects (morals, theology, social work).

Popular Movement (political)

It would not be difficult to list the works and the activities carried out in these years by the Popular Movement (MP): centers of solidarity, cultural centers, CUSL (University Cooperative for School and Work). By now, it would not be impossible to trace an organic picture of the important perspectives that are open for the MP in Campania. But this is not the point. Clarifying first of all that the MP does not interest itself only in politics understood in the strict sense, what we want to promote is the cultural power which our movement bears even in politics. Which is that the goal of politics is to serve man in his integrity. Politics in so far as it is the most complete form of culture cannot hold back its fundamental preoccupation with man. Culture is always situated in an essential and necessary relationship to what man is. Now, man has fundamental needs and desires that tend to be censored by the mass media. The conception of life portrayed by the mass media, in fact, does not value man in his deepest nature. In this sense, the works that we carry out must serve man in his elementary needs, as an instrument of education in order to perceive the presence of an ultimate meaning in things, which for that very reason goes beyond things and beyond works. Today's society tends to flatten man; the oppressive presence of the state tends to incorporate everything, even conscience (power today claims to conquer even conscience).

Giussani said at Assago (February 6, 1987): "The mass media and schooling become instruments for the fierce instilling of determined desires and for the obliteration or extermination of others."

Power=the delineation of the common goal and the organization of things for its fulfillment.

Man=defined by the religious sense: a search for truth and for happiness, a need to live things starting from an adequate meaning, which is the answer to his expectations. It can seem strange but what we do should have a direct relation with this dimension (adequate meaning). Otherwise, it is worth nothing. This is not idealism, but a true realism.

Culture=critical and systematic awareness of reality starting from a determined criterion.

Politics=the most complete form of culture, because it tends to promote the good for men. The criterion is precisely this: service to humanity.

In the course of this year, a creeping dissatisfaction, an uneasiness, has dominated. When it seemed like everything was moving toward the better, that everything was in order, there came a sense of tired calmness. *Everything is going well, but am I?* Sometimes, in the worst cases, there emerges the absolutizing of a particular or a psychological breakdown, or still, the absence of enthusiasm in doing things. The School of Community, with its insistence on the person, has recently opened the wound, or has made me perceive how problematic is the absolutizing of the particular and the absence of enthusiasm. I have lived all this with pain. The good I encountered seemed to diminish. There seem to be two causes of this situation: 1) the influx of power, that is, of the chaos with which everything inevitably has to deal; 2) the blurred face of the Movement that is not a driving and clear image within the chaos described. Instead, desperation, reactivity, and fragmentation prevail. The path forward touches aspects that are also strictly personal: 1) to recover and maintain the meaning of daily life—banality is enough to destroy the personal dimension; 2) to increase my awareness of this influx of power; 3) to build creative relationships that contribute actively to the spreading of the Kingdom. This path fills the moments of the day. We understand personally that the companionship stretches toward a goal. This is the overcoming of loneliness.

Starting from the self
  —From the totality of our own experience
  —The capacity to observe ourselves

To start from the self, which allows us to enter into action, that is, to begin to live, does not mean immediately to turn our attention on the depth of our being, that is, on what is defined as elementary experience. A method of this type brings with it the risk of intellectualism, of reasoning on the structure of man. Instead, we must observe ourselves, catch ourselves off-guard in action. To start from the self means to start from the present which we are living. We enter into play when we start from the joy or the difficulty or from the pain that we are living, not from the static structure of man in general. I cannot speak about the fact I encountered, that unsettled me four years ago, if I have an exam in two weeks. I have to start from the worry I experience in the present in order to compare it with the experience I have encountered. What is stronger, the worry or the experience I have encountered? Does the experience I have encountered save man abstractly or is it a concrete possibility to live differently, that is, better, the two weeks before the exam? Or does the experience I have encountered count in some cases and not in others?

There is a basic skepticism that blocks the path, meaning that this experience has value for my life but does not have value, deep down, for the most intimate and personal problems that I am living. If our experience does not start from the particular, it is better to go listen to academic lectures. We have to put in play what is in our heart in a relationship, with intelligence. In any case, the point of departure to understand the religious sense is an attention to particulars, and the particulars, more than just the affairs of CUSL, are also and above all the difficulties, the joys, etc., that I am living in the present. As I am now.

The task for these days is thus to take up again the particular with the awareness of what we are, to ask ourselves again the meaning of the banality that we live.

What is necessary is to rediscover a new concreteness starting from the self and reawakening a simple gaze on this friendship that is for you the only possibility, even if you imagined something else.

This companionship does not promise you the automatic solution of problems, but it does offer you the possibility to live your affairs within a horizon that is wider and more human.

That is, to expect all aspects of one's life to become engaged, in order not to be alone. Prayer: that this anxiety will disappear in a belonging. That this belonging will grow as an authority in my life.

In the frequent phenomena of stardom (Sting, Duran Duran, and in sports and in film), we must know how to glimpse the structural need for something that is outside of the ordinary, that is unusual, new, attractive. Does this describe Christianity today? Is it energetic, persuasive, fascinating, authoritative? Is it not maybe reduced by the fact that it often sums up the whole of life in a precept? Is it possibly true that the majority of Christian educators are content to see kids start down a tranquil path? From here comes the lack of excitement and the drying out of the best part of man.

We must begin the year with a radical question. It is radical because it touches the root of the person. The first words that we pronounce this year are that life, just as it is, is still too little. What contemporary culture teaches us is something else. They have told us that to have a big question, a great hope for a new, different life is something for kids. The moment we face real existence, little by little reality reveals its difficult and prosaic aspects. The dreams of childhood cloud over and disappear. We have to accept *daily life* with serenity, a daily life which settles down and defines itself (stepping out of the indeterminate and anxious tension) with the assigning of certain limits and laws, a precise goal, a well-defined and modest function. The big questions do not have any answer nor any possibility of being fulfilled. This is not the case for us:

we do not want to censor anything, most of all this deep desire that constitutes our person. This year has to begin with a radical question. In the companionship there is the answer to this desire, because the answer exists where you have glimpsed it, even if only for a moment. And that is here and nowhere else. (Anyway, there is no answer if there is not a big question: "Nothing is more absurd than an answer to a question that one has not asked"—Reinhold Niebuhr). Ours is not a work of poetic tension that lasts a moment, because there is a relationship between the *strong desire* and the circumstances of life. I would not get up in the morning in a hurry, nor would I study six hours a day, nor would I come to this parish, nor would I have the patience I have, if there was not a content on which my life rested. The day that you begin tomorrow is either an arid movement with some modest satisfaction, or it is an effort that has a specific outcome, the outcome of personal growth.

In order to have a true gaze toward persons and things, we need to eliminate the gods which we artificially set up. The moment they are destroyed, there should come, in order not to collapse, the emergence of the Goal. We cannot try to save our image or our future. Sometimes we search for some value that is partial and built by us because the height seems too far and requires effort.

Morality

We must always do our best in everything without the fear of pride. Humility will come through the circumstances that, perhaps, will displace you from the center of the situation. The circumstances are what dictate the law. It is not your mind that determines good and evil. The way you place yourself in front of the circumstances that present themselves is important, either to accept them or refuse them.

Ascesis

The certainty of the possibility of *ascesis* in facing circumstances is given by the fact that God does nothing by chance and thus chooses for you the most favorable conditions in order that *ascesis* may happen, and in the right way.

That you have to study Italian literature.
That you find yourself in front of your grandmother.
That you have to deal with noise.
That you have to deal with the parish.
That you have to deal with sadness.

On the Cultural Center

1) Something absolutely new happened: **the loss of the sense of the Mystery**. The epoch in which we live is a completely secularized epoch—the actions we carry out do not have any connection to destiny. The horizon is restricted to what we live. Philosophically, all this is said with an expression, "the death of God "(Nietzsche), meant obviously not in a literal sense. The lived reality of transcendence and providence have disappeared.

2) Today, instead, nihilism dominates. It takes on a form that is sometimes tragic (Pavese), sometimes minimalist (the shows on TV are made to forget and to distract, *life is all here*—what a narrow perspective! Nor do we recognize it. A healthy and conscious passion is needed. As in a song by Zuchero, "Only a healthy and conscious passion can save the young.")

3) In the serious world, instead, there are so-called values. And here, the discourse is insidious, because many Catholics eat this stuff up. Profit, efficiency, organization, well-being: these are the only values that can and must be recognized. Or: justice, peace, brotherhood. But are these values persuasive? A reasonable motivation is missing, a reason for which these values should be respected. Moreover, if they were respected, they would not for that reason be adequate to the desire of man. Secularization.

4) What is missing is not an idea, but a Fact that is exhilarating (for example, a mother, a girl, not philosophy). We

have to understand the level at which the Christian Fact is posed! (Like a baby who is born.) From here, the value of the Church. For this reason, without the content of the first chapter of *The Religious Sense*, we cannot understand Christianity.

a) The passage from myth, from prophecy, to the historical Fact: truth that is repeated, but anyway connected to Being and not to becoming. The forms of traditional religiosity speak about a distant god. Such distance is filled by rites, hopes, prophecies, idols. Christianity speaks about a present Reality, not about myths, etc.

b) The goal that we propose with the Cultural Center is to live with awareness, seeking not to be deceived and respecting our nature, the world of today, the air that we breathe. The attack by the world is fierce, though the manner is gentle, all about **usury, lust, power** (T.S. Eliot).

c) Augustine: Reason pushes us to do cultural work (which does not mean philosophical or research work). We must equip ourselves in front of the big attack. We must be strong and armed with reason in front of a culture that is consuming man. An adequate position is reasonable; we cannot resist the bombardment of today without equipping ourselves. A position is not adequate if, for example, it limits itself to caring for one's own soul in a sentimental way, without being capable of giving a judgment after reading an article. We need reasons that are adequate to the circumstances.

The circumstances we are living are characterized by what can be defined in various ways: nihilism or secularization.
The content of contemporary culture.
The need for radicality: *yes, yes; no, no.*

— Only having in front of ourselves, in fact, a greater reality, overcomes any type of anxiety. From here comes the importance of memory.

— Remembering makes us rediscover the unity of the self and thus order.

— The unity is beyond multiplicity, which is characterized by anxiety and worry. These things disperse us, fragment us.

Dante & **Saint Augustine** ("Late have I loved you…")

— The disappearance of this greater reality in individual life coincides with the loss of the taste for life. (We live between being and nothingness. But *nothing* ontologically does not exist; it exists only as an existential experience.)

— Memory makes man strong, unbeatable. It is the evocation of the only reality that embraces everything since it is the origin and end of everything. This reality does not require anything impossible. It does not go away, that is, it is not connected to the instability of empirical existence. It can always be called on again. It is, in fact, the meaning of everything.

* The non-obviousness of what we have said is in this: **In fact**, the escape hatch of our problems is somewhere else—in a voluntaristic effort to flatten things (the outcome is anxiety); in a tolerance of pain (a resignation without a total faith, which is thus skeptical).

* We do not need to chase after the truth, but to accept it, recognize it, evoke it. It is human to think only about having fun if we have not encountered a reality that is more true and more beautiful. It is human to remember if this encounter has taken place. Moralism is a kind of forcing: to follow a reality that is not the most beautiful and the most true because of a mental scheme.

— Starting from the self, realism.

— The unsuspected possibility of familiarity, even in boredom, with the meaning of things, with a friend.

— The place is the companionship, but there are a thousand ways of living in this companionship and only one that is authentic. For example, the one that makes you perceive, alone or in company, that there is one thing greater than all thoughts and worries—every instant is a decision of faith.

What moves us. Values? **A fact**. The dimension of ideas vs. the dimension of events. The idea of the mother vs. the mother herself. The sentimental pressure of values vs. the fullness and integrity of the Fact.

— Something persuasive is missing. (The death of God. Nihilism—tragic and minimalist).

— The persistence of ethical values and their insufficiency. (Liberal Catholicism.) Multiplicity (crisis of the modern world).

— The Christian Fact is integral and reasonable.

— The Fact that arises and the re-foundation of values.

— The gaze on the past. (Roots. The Middle Ages.)

Implications: without the comparison with an objective Fact, something that is beyond mere words, there are only opinions and dialectic.

"Better to adore a piece of straw that exists rather than a god deprived of reality" (Saint Augustine).

This is the only epoch in which the sense of the Mystery has been lost. We have arrived here thanks to a process of secularization: "God is dead" (Nietzsche). Many live today in an absence of references, of connections. Being a man means the need to connect yourself to something; lacking this, there is only confusion. The image of man in a river.

1) Obscured knowledge. Distant nostalgia. European man is intrigued by Christianity but does not adhere.
2) Ethical dispersion: the heart is like a stone. A body in relation is lacking.
   a) Authority is lacking (in the democratic era, this loses all value: there are authorities deprived of authority, deprived of fascination; only true authority moves us).
   b) A rule is lacking (because laxity is exalted). We do not know what to do.
3) Anthropological consequences
   a) The taste for living—a unified past. Beauty is lacking (the true and the beautiful coincide).
   b) Perfect systems—a refuge (a world turned upside down—Marx).
   c) Time—a unifying sense.
   d) Loneliness (absence of possession)—a life ordered to meaning.
   e) Voluntarist commitment—an objective goal is lacking.
   f) The State is the bulwark of confusion. The institutions tranquilize the soul.

The origin of power: the sufficient motive is **the will to power**. We need to take up again **the Nietzschean idea of the superman**, the man who is disenchanted, autonomous, the creator of new values. A clear example is given by Scalfari. The condition for power to be exercised is the obscuring of the person, who is the foundation of **freedom**. The heart is sacred. That is, it has to do with God. If there is not this link with God, man is lost, a prey of the winds, a victim of a biological or sociological mechanism, like a stone dragged along by the water. We can imagine this liberation from power as a boat with **a rope that is tied to an anchor**: even if he finds himself in stormy waters—and the contemporary epoch is comparable to a storm—he is not lost. The instrument

Joyful Days Ahead

that allows this link with God is regard for the heart ("**Tepidity** has never met God"—Blessed Simone Fidati). But the first act is grace. Man does not see the anchor. The concession to power happens today very often through a weakness of conscience: **an image is lacking**, a social body, a driving force (or at least this is reduced to a small light); the only real image is fashion. The time of poverty (Heidegger). The resolution is to create more society and less State.

Too many questions? Too big for the mind, too abstract for daily life? What has the study of the School of Community generated?

There is a kind of position within which we are consumed (perennial dissatisfaction): taking refuge in the desire of something that we do not have instead of returning to the present Reality that asks only to be reawakened. There is a kind of position in front of life where we are never satisfied; there is always something particular built by our mind or present in reality, but absolutized and that, because it is not realized, makes us sick. One is in high school and wants to be at university; one is at university and wants to return to high school; one is with a girl and desires freedom; one is freed and desires a girlfriend. There is a certain concreteness that has been lost: reality is that which should be.

— Never being satisfied with anything is human. Instead, it is inhuman to chase after things. Not being satisfied is the most evident sign that man is made for something greater than what he has in front of him. What you have in front of you is not enough for you; therefore, you take refuge in your thoughts.

> — We are together not to take refuge in thoughts, in desires, but to draw nearer to the only Reality that fills man's desire in the present. Only in a familiarity with what is greater than us do we find peace in the moment.

> — Only starting from a perspective of the religious sense, of the full awareness of the self, do we not waste time. But the religious sense, that series of questions, is exalted and sustained only within a companionship. The task of this week

is to re-evaluate this fabric of relationships. Everything is in service of this: the booth on campus, CUSL, CP (Cattolici Popolari[19]). Therefore, it does not have to do with a poetic or philosophical reflection.

— The particular is not lost. The religious question is excessive only because of your narrow perspective. We have to risk something in order to live relationships more deeply. Spiritual Exercises: we surrender in front of the smallest difficulty.

— Spiritual Exercises: reality calls you; we need a reasonable attitude.

— The work of the Cultural Center has re-opened the horizon.

— The problematic attitude closes me in. Seriousness: desire for fullness. Participation in a Fact. Gratuitous work.

— The effort to search for what makes you alive within things pushes you to reflect also on the things that would be easy to ignore.

— The Reasons are within a history; the connections are strengthened within the testimony that we make together.

A perspective that is certain: "Seek first the Kingdom ...and all these things will be given you besides" (*Matthew* 6:33). This is the definition of a goal. The character of this goal is: "the one who seeks, finds" (*Luke* 11:10). The dispersion of goals is the plodding along, trying to reach what can be lost. To follow what immediately pleases us generates anxiety, because we want to possess what can be lost, what we are already losing. The reduction *ad unum* (the one thing necessary) is the concentration that avoids getting lost and confused. It responds to the human need for recollection and openness to the infinite. The two extremes touch each other; in order to open ourselves to everything we need to settle down into ourselves. It is a sure perspective that dispossesses you of yourself.

19. An Italian political movement inspired by Communion & Liberation.

Joyful Days Ahead

Renunciation. The one who loses himself finds himself. The individualistic project creates a tranquility, a peaceful horizon, and faith suggests a suspicion, unveils the hidden cracks, makes us lose tranquility. On the other hand, faith launches us on a new horizon, unknown and incomprehensible, objective, but secure. It opens up another option.

We need a horizon of presentiment (intuition) in order to understand and live.

The way of reawakening the ultimate question is the way of reawakening the heart in the impact with reality, without censoring anything—without censoring the unrepeatable occasion that is offered to you to make your contribution, in total respect for your person, according to the condition in which you find yourself. This is a work that seeks to verify itself in the comparison, in a testimony.

I have the impression that every gesture of mine springs directly from faith and I am aware of it. It is like there is no longer anything between me and God.

Easter Spiritual Exercises of the University Students of Communion and Liberation
March 31–April 1, 1988
Certosa di Pavia, Italy

Luigi Giussani: I received a few passages from the writings of Giovanni Calzone, which his sister gave to me, and it seems to me that we are called to listen to his words. The posture that we should adopt in front of our destiny, and therefore in front of this companionship that destiny himself *made* in becoming man, found a witness in the short life of our friend Giovanni. Therefore, it is on these brief (for now) notes that we will develop our meditation. It is an inheritance, in fact, as the death and resurrection of Christ is an inheritance for our life.

A few months before he died, he wrote, "Joyful days are ahead because I have asked the Lord to be able to serve Him." They are not joyful days because he had finished university in a brilliant way, not because he was one of the most fascinating and *impressive* people of our companionship, not because he had in front of him a rich and totally positive future, not because he had a beautiful girlfriend (in fact he did have all of these): "Joyful days are ahead because I have asked the Lord to be able to serve Him." In this moment, heaven and earth, the past and the future, make the instant we are living dense, because in front of this truth we are normally empty, we are so far from this truth which is the goal of everything that exists, the goal of the earth we walk on, of the moment that passes, of the future, of the project that animates and gives flesh and form to our personality. Our thoughts and our love have only one goal. My thought and your thought, my love and your love, the love of any man and the thought of any man have only one goal: to serve the Lord. Thus, his death, the death of Giovanni—for those who knew him and for all of us, because through his witness I hope that we can all know him—is something that becomes great, becomes always greater, the more we think about it.

I am talking about something that in itself is so banal, because every day tens, hundreds of thousands of people die. But this is a man who recognized that the goal of living is to serve the Lord, that the goal of work and of love is to serve the Lord, that the goal of living and dying is to serve the Lord… to serve the Lord. We belong to a destiny, to a destiny that is not ours, that we do not make, and this destiny, this great design to which we belong, insignificant dust that we are, became a man who put himself by our side as a companion in life. The fact is that God, that the word *God* bursts forth from our hearts and our eyes, so that we can penetrate with our faces and our hearts the breath of the Mystery! Everything depends, everything hangs on this; everything is a part of His will. This destiny, this design, this Mystery became a man, our companion, just like the person who is sitting next to you right now is a companion. Let us listen to the Word of the Gospel.

Reading: The 72 returned rejoicing, and said, "Lord, even the demons are subject to us because of your name." Jesus said, "I have observed Satan fall like lightning from the sky. Behold, I have given you the power to tread upon serpents and scorpions and upon the full force of the enemy and nothing will harm you. Nevertheless, do not rejoice because the spirits are subject to you, but rejoice because your names are written in heaven." (*Luke* 10:17–20)

Giussani: Do not rejoice because you have reason and intelligence and, in the time that passes, with the inevitable connections that intertwine and solidify, you will make progress. What is progress? Be happy because you have God as a friend and companion.

Reading: As they continued their journey, he entered a village where a woman whose name was Martha welcomed Him. She had a sister named Mary who sat beside the Lord at His feet listening toHim speak. Martha, burdened with much serving, came to Him and said, "Lord, do you not care that my sister has left me by myself to do the serving? Tell her to help me." The Lord said to her in reply, "Martha, Martha, you are anxious and worried about many things. There is need of only one thing. Mary has chosen the better part and it will not be taken from her." (*Luke* 10:38–42)

Giussani: There is a point, a point in the horizon of the heart, that is the center of everything. There is a substance of feeling—and first, and therefore more profoundly—there is a substance of memory and of thought that is the center of the world and therefore of our life. The difference between Mary and Martha is that Mary is amazed in front of this point, because even she had to prepare something to eat, even she had to act as her sister acted. What immense activity stirs in the universe! But there is a relationship, a relationship that is immensely, immeasurably more valid, greater, more imposing, without equal, than everything that moves in the universe. There is no kind of relationship greater than this one: the relationship with Christ. What is there about this relationship in your life? It is not a negation of anything. Every ant takes its step and every human thought vibrates according to the direction of this relationship. There is not even a leaf that can fall without returning to the design that is this Man. It is the comparison and relationship with this Man that gives meaning to the leaf that falls, to the thought that vibrates, and to the ant that walks. What place does He have in your life, in my life, this One who came? "Emmanuel," who came to be with me, a companion for my life. What a terrible thing is this stone dryness that most of the time is the attitude in our heart! Today it is like a question, a humble supplication. We pray that this stone may be broken by the sweetness of His memory, by the sweetness of His name: *Dulcis Christe*.

Dulcis Christe [Sweet Christ] (by Michelangelo Grancini, 1605–1669).

Now let us follow the path that our friend marked with his reflection and in which each of us already participates in our reflections, so that, step by step, everything may become meaningful in the light of a word that renews a judgment and reanimates a hope. "The problem," Giovanni says, "is to find something on which we can fix our attention in order to overcome our difficulties." Life is difficult, it is full of difficulties. The challenge is to find an element on which to focus attention for the overcoming of these difficulties. "I need to focus on these areas [everyday]: study, perfectionism [the need for perfection or a moralistic preoccupation], introversion, pensiveness [which corrodes], scrupulosity, vigilance, gossip. For each of these things I need to pay particular attention." When memory is fixed on one of these areas, on a preoccupation, then everything closes up; my life rests on all these little pieces. Life is a tangle of difficulties, of remaining caught up in problems to resolve. How can we attempt to overcome these difficulties? Life is a tangle of difficulties, not necessarily dramatic, but like a web, like a mesh of difficulties—not something we even think about, but a tangle of difficulties. Let us listen to what the Gospel says.

Reading: At the sight of the crowds, His heart was moved with pity for them because they were troubled and abandoned, like sheep without a shepherd. Then He said to His disciples, "The harvest is abundant but the laborers are few; so ask the master of the harvest to send out laborers for His harvest." (*Matthew* 9:36–38)

Giussani: They were like sheep without a shepherd. Our days are like a flock of preoccupations and difficulties without a guide. And so, life is like a quiet war.

"La guerra" ["The War"] (by Claudio Chieffo, 1945–2007).

So, the circumstances are key, because the difficulties hide in the circumstances. This means that the difficulties come at random; life is abandoned to chance. Circumstances define our horizon: if, as Giovanni told us before, an area of worry grabs our attention and we fix our gaze on it, the horizon of our life is the circumstance that gives us that worry. The circumstances define our horizon. We are blocked and pulled by the circumstances. We are blocked and at the same time pulled, dissolved by circumstances, like Giovanni said in his text: "Our pain stems from the fact that we have come to live outside the horizon [the true and fulfilled horizon] of the sacred. Our everyday horizon changes with the change of circumstances. But the horizon that is defined by the circumstances is suffocating; attractive at the beginning, it then becomes boring. Living within this type of horizon, we adjust and try to put the pieces of ourselves in order. But the numbers never add up." At one time in the dust, at another time in the fire, at another time under water—the circumstances lead us where they will, like the Lord told us.

Reading: On the next day, when they came down from the mountain, a large crowd met Him. There was a man in the crowd who cried out, "Teacher, I beg you, look at my son; he is my only child. For a spirit seizes him and he suddenly screams and it convulses him until he foams at the mouth; it releases him only with difficulty, wearing him out. I begged your disciples to cast it out but they could not." (*Luke* 9:37–40)

Giussani: So too, our life is marked by uncontrollable upheavals, in a very grave form, in a form that is even normal, and in fact no one pays attention to it anymore…It is not true that no one pays attention to it, because God came and became our companion in order to tear us away from this useless convulsion that closes and at the same time disperses us. And it is in this continual change brought about by slavery to the circumstances, in this continual change brought about by anxiety, by worry, or by difficulties, that breathlessness and fatigue weigh on life, such that the only divinity that frees us is distraction. *O anime affaticate* (O weary souls)...

"Anime affaticate et sitibonde" ["Tired Souls, Searching"] (by Francesco Soto de Langa, 1534–1619)

Therefore, Giovanni says passionately: "Is there a center on which I can place my attention, concentrate my energy, to avoid being dispersed in a multitude of areas [of thought, of worry, of difficulty], and which, at the same time, allows me to walk a path that encompasses everything [because I do not want to lose anything], without leaving anything out? [Does this center exist?] I need, at this point, to expand upon that Christian hypothesis: 'Seek first the Kingdom and His righteousness and all these things will be given you besides.'" Because "the waters of Egypt are cloudy and bitter." "Woe to you rich," says the Gospel.

Reading: "But woe to you who are rich, for you have received your consolation. But woe to you who are filled now, for you will be hungry. Woe to you who laugh now, for you will grieve and weep. Woe to you when all speak well of you, for their ancestors treated the false prophets in this way." (*Luke* 6:24–26)

At that time, some people who were present there told Him about the Galileans whose blood Pilate had mingled with the blood of their sacrifices. He said to them in reply, "Do you think that because these Galileans suffered in this way they were greater sinners than all other Galileans? By no means! But I tell you, if you do not repent, you will all perish as they did! Or those 18 people who were killed when the tower at Siloam fell on them—do you think they were more guilty than everyone else who lived in Jerusalem? By no means! But I tell you, if you do not repent, you will all perish as they did!" (*Luke* 13:1–5)

Giussani: Saint Teresa of Ávila, in her great prayer that we will now sing, understood this profoundly, so much so that her life was determined and dominated by it. But one dies, if she does not let herself die in the arms of this center, because to rest upon this center, to rest on Christ can seem like a loss from the human point of view. But Giovanni said, "... without leaving anything out," without losing anything. In this paradox, our life is called to discovery and to the most evocative adventure, because we will die if we do not die on this center.

"Moro, perche non moro" ["I Die Because I Don't Die"] (based on the text of Saint Teresa of Ávila, 1515–1582)

"Even though we can sometimes fool ourselves into believing that we need something now that is objectively illusory," says Giovanni, "even though we can sometimes fool ourselves into believing that we need something now that is objectively illusory [ephemeral], still, we cannot fool ourselves about our desire for life, a desire that is disturbed by the thought of death. Here it becomes clear that only God can resolve this problem." He wrote this a few days before his death: "What will man give in exchange for himself?"

Reading: When they came to Capernaum, the collectors of the temple tax approached Peter and said, "Doesn't your teacher pay the temple tax?" "Yes," he said. When he came into the house, before he had time to speak, Jesus asked him, "What is your opinion, Simon? From whom do the kings of the earth take tolls or census tax? From their subjects or from foreigners?" When he said, "From foreigners," Jesus said to him, "Then the subjects are exempt." (*Matthew* 17:24–26)

Giussani: It would be so clear, if only we could see it, but in man clarity comes from reason, from conscience, from the heart. So if we give credit to this vision of reason, of conscience, of the heart, we begin to see also with our eyes, but if we could see, it would seem easy to understand. This is the sadness.

"Ballata dell'uomo vecchio" ["Ballad of the Old Man"] (by Claudio Chieffo, 1945–2007)

Our desire for life, which is upset by death and which only God can "resolve," as our friend Giovanni said, changes, all of a sudden and totally, the context, the structure, because God made Himself familiar. And so, our daily life has the possibility of becoming familiar with the meaning of everything, with destiny. Maybe this is the most profound and beautiful phrase: "If the possibility of familiarizing ourselves with the meaning of everything does not exist, how can we live? The strong man is the one who, after any adversity, returning to himself, recognizes a meaning that envelops the event. If I, after anything that happens to me, returning to myself, do not have the capacity to say truly, 'I belong' ['in what happened, I belong to You'] and in this pronouncement to find my peace, or at least to glimpse it, I am still immature [a nonman]. The possibility of maturity is linked to the existence of the sign." Everything is a sign. That everything is a sign means that, in everything, we are face-to-face with our destiny, because if what we do is a sign, within it our destiny is therefore present to us in everything that we do—present to us in what we do. "The possibility of maturity is linked to the existence of the sign and the instrument that carries with it an objective Meaning." That is, everything that we do is an instrument that carries, that brings, an objective meaning. This is not an abstract word by a philosopher or by a man who thinks confusedly as a man. The possibility of maturity is connected to the existence of Christ recognized within everything; the possibility of maturity is connected to the existence of things recognized as an instrument that makes Christ present. To familiarize ourselves with the Mystery is for Him to become our daily bread. To familiarize ourselves with Christ is the daily bread that we find in everything that we accomplish, a food and a drink that fills our hunger and thirst continually.

Reading: When the crowd saw that neither Jesus nor His disciples were there, they themselves got into boats and came to Capernaum looking for Jesus. And when they found Him across the sea they said to Him, "Rabbi, when did you get here?" Jesus answered them and said, "Amen, amen, I say to you, you are looking for me not because you saw signs but because you ate the loaves and were filled. Do not work for food that perishes but for the food that endures for eternal life, which the Son of Man will give you. For on Him the Father, God, has set His seal." So they said to Him, "What can we do to accomplish the works of God?" Jesus answered and said to them, "This is the work of God, that you believe in the one he sent." So they said to Him, "What sign can you do, that we may see and believe in you? What can you do? Our ancestors ate manna in the desert, as it is written: 'He gave them bread from heaven to eat.'" So Jesus said to them, "Amen, amen, I say to you, it was not Moses who gave the bread from heaven; my Father gives you the true bread from heaven. For the bread of God is that which comes down from heaven and gives life to the world." So they said to Him, "Sir, give us this bread always." Jesus said to them, "I am the bread of life; whoever comes to me will never hunger, and whoever believes in me will never thirst. But I told you that although you have seen me, you do not believe. Everything that the Father gives me will come to me, and I will not reject anyone who comes to me, because I came down from heaven not to do my own will but the will of the one who sent me. And this is the will of the one who sent me, that I should not lose anything of what he gave me, but that I should raise it on the last day. For this is the will of my Father, that everyone who sees the Son and believes in Him may have eternal life, and I shall raise him on the last day." (*John* 6:24–40)

Giussani: We eat and drink, which means we get our fill of what happens to us, but what happens to us would not have meaning, ephemeral and illusory as it is, if it were not part of a design, if it were not the sign of a meaning. This design, this meaning, became a man. This is what differentiates us from everyone in the world: faith, which means the recognition of this Presence in which what we eat and drink, waking and sleeping, living and dying, "are within this relationship with you, O Christ." "You do not believe"; "no, Lord, we believe; we believe in order to live in familiarity with you, O Christ." This is the absolutely gratuitous thing, outside of any type of interest, that should introduce itself in your life. Therefore, we cannot be understood—in this desire, in this recognition, in this adoration, in this tenderness, in this familiarity, in this dedication—we can never be understood, even by that part of ourselves that continues to remain part of the world. Of the world means, of that which hates Him, that which cannot receive Him, that cannot welcome Him. "He came to His own, but His own did not welcome Him." This is the meaning of the message that our Easter poster gives us to meditate on. Now let us listen to it again, slowly. How many times must we look at it, how many times must we look at it putting this phrase in front of our eyes, in front of our face, because it is in us that something must happen in the relationship with Him, "in the relationship with You, O Christ." Let us read, then, let us listen to this passage that we have already read in *Il Sabato*, but which comes from *A Short Story of the Anti-Christ* by Soloviev.

Reading: Now, in a grieved voice, the Emperor addressed them: "What else can I do for you, you strange people? What do you want from me? I cannot understand. Tell me yourselves, you Christians, deserted by the majority of your peers and leaders, condemned by popular sentiment. What is it that you value most in Christianity?" At this, Elder John rose up like a white candle and answered quietly: "Great sovereign! What we value most in Christianity is Christ Himself—in His person. All comes from Him, for we know that in Him dwells the whole fullness of the Godhead bodily." (Vladimir Soloviev, *A Short Story of the Anti-Christ*, 1900)

Giussani: "You strange people...tell me yourselves, you Christians, deserted by the majority of your peers and leaders: What is it that you value most in Christianity?" Then Elder John got up and answered quietly: "Great sovereign! What we value most in Christianity is Christ Himself—in His person. All comes from Him [that is, everything], for we know that in Him dwells all the fullness of the Godhead bodily [physically!]." The meaning and the consistency of everything. "He Himself and everything that comes from Him." What comes from Him? Everything. "Even the hairs of your head have been numbered" (*Matthew* 10:30). "We can see you, O Christ, like old Simeon saw you in his arms," as our great teacher Péguy tells us in *The Portal of the Mystery of Hope*. But there is an objection to this message, to the endurance of this message, because heaven and earth will pass away, but this message will not pass away: "I am with you always until the end of the world" (*Matthew* 28:20). The objection is pain, but it is not an objection, it is not an objection—it is a pain that the condition of this relationship is pain. There is an aspect of pain, the greatest space that pain occupies in our life, the most dangerous, because it is the most centrifugal: it is fear, the fear that in following Christ in this life of familiarity with Him we do not know what will happen. The difference with other men is that they, in those moments, in those few moments when they think of their future, they are terrified; but they remain liberated thanks to their eternal, stubborn, humiliating distraction, because for them the circumstances are the circle in which they are enclosed, as we saw before. But our eyes have been opened and doing the will of God, as Giovanni said, can mean that after two days one can be asked for his very life. There is a passage from the Gospel that we should listen to.

Reading: He said to His disciples, "Therefore I tell you, do not worry about your life and what you will eat, or about your body and what you will wear. For life is more than food and the body more than clothing. Notice the ravens: they do not sow or reap; they have neither storehouse nor barn, yet God feeds them. How much more important are you than birds! Can any of you by worrying add a moment to your life-span? If even the smallest things are beyond your control, why are you anxious about the rest? Notice how the flowers grow. They do not toil or spin. But I tell you, not even Solomon in all his splendor was dressed like one of them. If God so clothes the grass in the field that grows today and is thrown into the oven tomorrow, will he not much more provide for you, O you of little faith? As for you, do not seek what you are to eat and what you are to drink, and do not worry anymore. All the nations of the world seek for these things, and your Father knows that you need them. Instead, seek His kingdom, and these other things will be given you besides." (*Luke* 13:22–31)

Giussani: "If God so clothes the grass in the field that grows today and is thrown into the oven tomorrow, will he not much more provide for you, O you of little faith?" "How much more important are you than birds!" If pain is imagination, that is, if pain is fear of the future, this pain is so easily—we have to say this to ourselves—alleviated by the Word of the Gospel. One of Giovanni's words reminds us of the density that pain can have in the present. He writes, "Pain in the present reveals the heart by enlarging it." I understand; at your age I did not understand. How many years had to pass so that I could realize one day, while I was in the car talking with someone, that without suffering a relationship is not true. Without suffering, our possession, our relationship is not true; without suffering nothing is true. What does it mean that a relationship becomes true in suffering? It means that in suffering that relationship assumes its place in the total design and the heart grows larger. In that relationship, the heart embraces everything, everything. We cannot love a person, or a thing, without embracing the totality that it serves or of which it is a sign. "Pain in the present reveals the heart by enlarging it." Let us imagine what the pain in the heart of Christ revealed, what kind of greatness in the heart of Christ, when he turned and saw the people that followed Him and had pity on them, because they were like sheep without a shepherd. Or that time when, together with the apostles—the Samaritan woman had gone away—looking at the fields with a gaze that maybe was sad and full of desire, said, "The harvest is abundant but the laborers are few. So ask the master of the harvest…" (*Matthew* 9:37-38); or the moment when they came upon Him weeping… Christ, destiny made man who weeps in front of His city. "Pain in the present reveals the heart by enlarging it."

Reading: As he drew near, he saw the city and wept over it, saying, "If this day you only knew what makes for peace—but now it is hidden from your eyes. For the days are coming upon you when your enemies will raise a palisade against you; they will encircle you and hem you in on all sides. They will smash you to the ground and your children within you, and they will not leave one stone upon another within you because you did not recognize the time of your visitation." (*Luke* 19:41-44)

Giussani: "Because you did not recognize the time of your visitation." But the greatness of the heart with which Christ embraced, in His gaze, the city and its tragic future, symbol of the tragic future of the world, which He had to experience when he died a few days later, this great heart, within the gaze that embraces everything, looks also at my city, is looking at your city, the city of your life, your world, the world of your I.

The Greek word that is behind the translation we just heard should be translated in a much more intense way than with the words "he wept." It should be, "he sobbed." Let us stop to look at that Man who says those words: "You did not recognize the time of your visitation." Each of us is called to participate in the greatness of that heart. But there is another aspect of suffering, the darkest aspect, the gloomy aspect of pain, the aspect where pain becomes a synonym for injustice, suffering as the fruit of violence, suffering as the fruit of hatred, that is, suffering as the monster that is born from a lie. Suffering as the fruit of violence, as a projection of hatred and of lies... Tomorrow, above all tomorrow, we will be called to this dimension of memory, but I want to recall it now for each of us, because we cannot become familiar with Christ, we cannot live our faith in Christ, in Christ, we cannot be companions with Him and accept Him as a companion on our path, we cannot be understood, we cannot be tolerated in our affirmation that He accompanies us in daily life. At the heart of the struggle, which especially in these moments has reached a level never reached before... no, never before, because in '75, in '76, and in '77, it was roughly the same...all the enmity, the hostility, all the calumny, (because the only weapon is calumny and invectiveness); all this they use against us. We do well to be attentive not to let ourselves be fooled. We have some idea, but the reason is here; the reason is in the hatred, the violent hatred born of a lie, because "the world is the son of the devil," Christ said. The hatred that produces violence is the fruit of the lie, because it cannot be bearable and tolerable that in the life of society a man can say, "Christ is with us." The meaning of everything, destiny, is with us; everything must refer to Him, He is the source of the judgment on everything and each person is responsible in front of Him. There is no other power because the only power is His. Everything is just, even earthly power, if it is responsible in front of Him and He is the prince of liberty: "The truth will set you free," because He is the truth, because He is the prince of liberty. The supreme sign is that the work that He "becomes" in the world, His mysterious body that grows in history, finds space, the necessary space, the necessary recognition. And instead no, the Church is persecuted, the truth of the Church is intolerable for today's mentality. In short, this is what is behind the struggle against the vicar of Christ and his infallible word: the Pope. It is a tremendous honor, under which our timidity seems crushed, that of having become the pretext for the attack of the world and of the lie against the truth: "Tell me yourselves, you Christians, deserted by the majority of your peers and leaders." It is not only the pain of a sacrifice that expands the heart, that uncovers and expands the heart, but it is above all the pain of the lie, the pain of the hatred, the pain of the violence against our life. This is the inevitable condition of familiarity with Christ when it is recognized and embraced. It was the destiny of the apostles, until, that is, they fled, *fugerunt*, they abandoned Him. They abandoned Him without abandoning Him in their heart, but they abandoned Him; socially they abandoned Him. It is an inevitable condition but it is an affirmation that is not reasonable, an affirmation that is wrong, it is called "lie." Our life, which is so fragile, so full of limits, so weak, so sinful, is called to defend the truth, is called to carry truth, that is, God, in the world.

Reading: "If the world hates you, realize that it hated me first. If you belonged to the world, the world would love its own; but because you do not belong to the world, and I have chosen you out of the world, the world hates you. Remember the word I spoke to you, 'No slave is greater than his master.' If they persecuted me, they will also persecute you. If they kept my word, they will also keep yours. And they will do all these things to you on account of my name, because they do not know the one who sent me. If I had not come and spoken to them, they would have no sin; but as it is they have no excuse for their sin. Whoever hates me also hates my Father. If I had not done works among them that no one else ever did, they would not have sin; but as it is, they have seen and hated both me and my Father. But in order that the word written in their law might be fulfilled, 'They hated me without cause.'" (*John* 15:18–25)

Giussani: There is a psalm, the second psalm, that has always been interpreted by rabbinic tradition as a messianic psalm, a psalm in which this destiny of God made man, who would be hated without reason, was proclaimed, foreseen, written about so many centuries before He came.

"*I re della terra*" ["The Kings of the Earth"] (based on *Psalm* 2)

But the world cannot defeat God. There is more humanity, more intelligence, more truth, more tenderness, more affection, more heart—it is more human to be with Christ. The pain that we imagine or the pain that reveals the heart, even the pain of the lie, that makes us strangers to our brothers, cannot be a reason to stop our adherence. This is what our friend Giovanni says with his incredible final testimony: "Living is never banal if we remember that the Infinite is mysterious and powerful and destroys all our idols [the circumstances that close in on us] even those that are most persuasive. There is always, in every instant, even if it does not seem to be the case, the possibility of transcending the sphere of the obvious and continuing on the second journey." The sphere of the obvious is the immediacy of what we see, what we touch, what we feel: the ephemeral. "There is always… the possibility of transcending the sphere of the obvious and continuing on the second journey." The first journey is the things that we touch, the hand that we grab, the eye that sees, but the second journey is that which comes soon after, sooner not later, within. It is the search for meaning, the discovery of reality as a sign, the reality that becomes, as it did for Dante's Ulysses, an ocean to navigate. "There is always, in every instant [in every moment with a book in front of you], even if it does not seem to be the case, the possibility of transcending the sphere of the obvious and continuing on the second journey. Everything exhausts itself. The Infinite does not. To open ourselves means to stand with an open mind, listening for that which all things hide." This is the Infinite as lived by a young man, this is the Infinite that a young man lives, our companion. Our companion: Christ is our companion, but the Infinite that is Christ becomes a dimension that is so evident in this stranger we run into at school, that it makes him also a companion like Christ. There is a difference, but there is no longer disunity, there is no longer separation: Christ or Giovanni. "To open ourselves [to breathe] means to stand with an open mind, listening for that which all things hide [everything is a sign]." "Living is no longer banal if we remember that the Infinite is mysterious and powerful and destroys" everything that is limited, even the most persuasive things.

"There is always, in every instant, even if it does not seem to be the case, the possibility of transcending the sphere of the obvious and continuing on the second journey. Everything exhausts itself. The Infinite does not. To open ourselves means to stand with an open mind, listening for that which everything hides." This is our life, it is the life to which we are called, and therefore you hide the Infinite, in you is the Infinite. With you, in you, I live the Infinite. To live, then, is no longer banal. "How much (how just and bitter a marvel this is) we are immersed in the mist," in the darkness, in the fog, with smoke in our eyes. "How much we are immersed in the mist of the obvious [the tangible] and of idols!!!"—that which we fix for ourselves. The passage of the Gospel of Saint John that we will now read, although short, is a comment on this phrase from Giovanni, because it is the most beautiful definition that I have read of the Infinite that is in daily life, of the Infinite that one like you is capable of.

Reading: "Amen, amen, I say to you, whoever believes in me will do the works that I do, and will do greater ones than these, because I am going to the Father. And whatever you ask in my name, I will do, so that the Father may be glorified in the Son. If you ask anything of me in my name, I will do it." (*John* 14:12–14)

Giussani: "Whoever follows me, whoever listens to me, will do the works I do, and will do greater ones than these." It is the greatness of Christ that enters into us, literally; it is the Infinite that enters into life, which otherwise is illusory. "The obvious and the idol, the banality and the suffocation that is constricting and small. But is it possible, is it really possible to live like this?" This phrase he wrote in his journal the day before his death: "I have the impression that every gesture of mine springs directly from faith and I am aware of it. It is like there is no longer anything between me and God." Is there anything greater, an event greater than a death like this? "I have the impression that every gesture of mine springs directly from faith"—faith, the recognition of a Presence. Faith is the recognition of a greater Presence, of the greater Presence. There is only one who is greater than man: the man Christ, the man God. "I have the impression that every gesture of mine springs directly from faith and I am aware of it. It is like there is no longer anything between me and God." "You have freed us, Lord. I adore You, Redeemer, liberator." "It is like there is no longer anything between me and God" – that is, one is free, free. I hope that it is easy for us to imagine the scene of this world for a man that talks like this, for each of us to talk like this: it is freedom. "I adore You, Redeemer."

"Ti adoro Redentore" ["I Adore You, Redeemer"] (by Antonio Martorell, 1913–2009)

Assembly of the Community of Communion and Liberation in Campania with Luigi Giussani

March 26, 1988

Naples

"Joyful days are ahead because I have asked the Lord to be able to serve Him" (Giovanni).

Speaker: We begin this meeting which we have anticipated with so much hope, because the dramatic events that we've lived in these last months have opened up the necessity not to put any more barriers, any more resistance in front of the event that is among us. Today's encounter aims to create a dialogue on how we have lived, on how we are living what has happened and what is happening, in such a way as to be able to pass from a sentimental position to a more open, deeper question in front of reality and life. Therefore, let us bring forward right away all there is to bring forward.

Luigi Giussani: First of all, I would like to express my gratitude to all of you for this possibility that you have given me, because I have desired this moment, ever since that day when other things kept me from coming to speak to you. Therefore, first of all, I am deeply grateful to you for this moment and for the hope which is always to be renewed—as a thought is always to be renewed and as freedom is always to be renewed. The difference between spirit, what we call "spirit," and what we call "matter" is that the spirit

Assembly of the Community of Communion and Liberation in Campania

is always "from the beginning," that is, always new, resurgent in the moment. This hope that is always to be renewed are Giovanni Calzone and Massimo Cioncada, who will always assure us of this hope and gratitude. The philosophers say that a being is there where it acts; one is there where he acts, where there is an action. This means that there is a subject. It will be their presence that makes itself an experience of the new fire that will continue to be placed in our hearts. We ask them to pray for us, now that they see each of us down to the marrow of our bones, now that they are present with a familiarity and a power that before they could only provoke indirectly. Now that they see us like this, they help us in the effort that is still left for us to make. I am very grateful to you.

Speaker: I would like your help to look at what is happening to me in this moment, so that what happens to me may not remain a simple emotion of the moment, but something that generates an attitude of life in me. When I met the friends of the Fraternity, I asked them about what was happening to me, because they helped me to live it. And it was this: what happened to me—Giovanni was very close to me, even beyond the fact that he was Pina's brother—provoked in me a really strong pain, but this pain seemed to re-shape, to re-dimension everything around me, all my life, all the obviousness of life. From this pain came an immediate desire, maybe one that is impulsive and emotional, to live differently. If a pain like this happened every day, a pain so moving for me, so capable of melting me, I would live daily life in a different way. After a week of work, it was as if I tried to distance myself from the fact. The first thing that came to my mind was to remind myself of the most painful moment, which was the announcement of what happened, when I cried. And it was this memory, this continuing to repeat it to myself, to remember what had happened, that particular, that kept the desire awake in me. I would like your help in this, because I want to understand where the emotion of the instant ends and where this pain brings out a true question for me.

Giussani: The pain of an instant ceases to have a purely sentimental significance when it changes life, when it changes something. And the word "re-dimension" that you used is so significant, because "to re-dimension" means "to give another measure to things." Therefore, you spoke rightly about wanting to live differently.

Pina has been so kind as to give me some passages from Giovanni that I have looked at now quickly. Some of this I already knew, but if each of us had these two pages in our daily diary, if we used them every day, it would be a great lesson, continually imparted by a friendship that cannot fail. If friendship is a companionship to destiny, these reflections and these notes that I have read are the best words of such a companionship. We need to hear our friend speak, we need to hear what he says. We know very well that someone can accompany us even in apparent silence. These phrases, though, lead us to a presence that is not silent, but vehemently like a question for our life. Therefore, our struggle should be against that type of life that tries to detach; to empty out the daily life that we are accustomed to. This is also the thought in a letter of Emmanuel Mounier, from which I will read a piece, commenting on a phrase of Giovanni at the last CLU Exercises that we had. Writing to his wife in a serious disgrace that had befallen them, Emmanuel Mounier says: "We need to oppose the kind of daily life that makes the wound habitual." We must not grow accustomed to it. But what conquers daily life in its capacity to numb us, to empty us out, that is—to say a terrible word—to forget? Man is that level where nature cannot forget, where everything unites in a perspective that has no end. The word that indicates the work to us—the work, because it is a commitment of our freedom—against the daily life that numbs us, is the word "memory." You have recalled for us, my friend, you have described well what this memory is. Speaking in a Christian way—Christian vocabulary takes the words of the common vocabulary, but does not limit them to how man normally uses them; it takes the words of the natural vocabulary and expands them to their ultimate meaning, giving them a fullness—we use the word "memory" as

Assembly of the Community of Communion and Liberation in Campania

Christ taught us, because the only commandment that he gave us to link our ephemeral moment to His permanence in history is the word *memory*: "Do this in memory of me." The word "memory," used in a Christian way, indicates a fact that began in the past, but is in the present, is present, is a present fact that began in the past. Thus, we will never lose, in eternity, our friendship and everything that has died and has become the content of our heart, of our awareness. I have asked to be able to pray with you, to say the Holy Mass with you, and therefore this moment surprises me, in the sense that it would be more beautiful if we re-read these phrases slowly. But maybe it will push you to read them for yourselves. First, anyway, we can never forget, every day, that "pain in the present reveals the heart by enlarging it." I hope that you are doing the School of Community! In the School of Community, what is the heart, this word that we have taken from the Bible? The heart indicates the place, so to speak, where man is identified by needs, desires, and evidences that are boundless. Man is that level of nature where nature becomes aware of an endless need, the need for an ultimate meaning, as Giovanni will say elsewhere. Suffering, which makes us experience the impossibility of satisfying these needs in time, pushes us either to cynicism or to admit, to recognize, the endless perspective which arises in each of us. This is the only thing that makes it reasonable for a mother to give birth: the existence of happiness for which the heart that is given to us is made, the conscious life that has been given to us. Suffering, making us face the limit in time and space, of the great search and of the great need of the heart, pushes us to understand the destiny for which we are made. And therefore, the more one lives this memory, the more one reflects on this, the more his life takes on new dimensions, assumes the right measure, that measure about which Giovanni spoke so well in another passage. He said, "Living is never banal if we remember that the Infinite is mysterious and powerful and destroys all our idols, even those that are most persuasive. There is always, in every instant, even if it does not seem to be the case, the possibility of transcending the sphere of the obvious and continuing on the second journey. [As I said at the Exercises, the second journey is the one that moves us toward destiny. What we feel with our hands and see with our eyes is simply, so to speak, the point of departure.] Everything exhausts itself. Only the Infinite endures. [The infinite is in the heart, is the dimension of the heart.] To open ourselves means to stand with an open mind, listening for that which all things hide. [And each thing beckons to infinite destiny. Therefore, everything hides in itself this relationship that should be continually "re-membered," taken up again. This is so true that he adds:] How much we are immersed in the mist [in the darkness] of the obvious and of idols [of the thing for its own sake]!!!"

Speaker: For us in CLU, in particular those who were closest to Giovanni, it is as if this wound that continually bleeds has brought us to a dimension that you have always mentioned, but that we are finally understanding now, that is, the dimension of the question. A whole series of needs, of questions, have come up that go beyond our desperation. These are a series of questions that have led us to ask Christ the meaning of what is happening to us and to live the relationship among us like this. For this reason, the relationship that we are living with Annarita [his fiancé], who is witnessing this to us with great freedom, has been truly amazing. I ask you, therefore, in this relationship, in this moment, what do we ask and how do we ask, how do we enter into relationship with this Infinite, so that this meaning can remain?

Giussani: How do you remain in relationship with this Infinite? Which means: how do you remain in relationship with Giovanni and Massimo? Which means: how do you remain in relationship with reality without losing it? Now, in the scientific field we say that a working hypothesis, a kind of forecast of a solution shows itself to be true, and therefore becomes a law, is recognized as a law, when it explains the phenomenon, retaining all of its aspects, when it explains the phenomenon and retains all its aspects. A hypothesis of life is right when it unfolds, explains, illuminates, retaining all the aspects, because this is the concept of reason. Reason is the awareness of reality according to the totality of its factors. Thus, an explanation, an answer to a question, however serious or heavy it may be, is right wherever it is a law, wherever your explanation retains all the aspects of the phenomenon, which in this case is life. Therefore, cynicism is always a lie, and desperation is always a lie. I quoted for you at the Exercises a great writer, a great Christian thinker, John Climacus, who said that penitence is resistance to desperation. Penitence in the Christian sense, which means rebirth, conversion, is resistance to desperation, because it is resistance to the supreme lie. Cynicism and desperation make us lose everything, they do not explain everything. Therefore, they have the effect of a lie—and a very understandable one, for the love of God! In any case, we need to stay close to each other in our companionship and be clear about this habit of thought. It is a great sickness, the most terrible sickness, without comparison, worse than death. The weakness of cynicism and desperation is not only a weakness. Everything within the horizon of our life, everything is essentially positive. All the traces of truth, of justice, of love, of joy, are the negation of the lie. Therefore, I believe, my friend, that we should ask, we should beg that the awareness of God become as familiar to us as I read in the pages of Giovanni: "I have the impression that every gesture of mine springs directly from faith and I am aware of it. It is like there is no longer anything between me and God." The measure of man is this, is this dimension to which we should re-dimension ourselves. We should ask for this dimension, that this dimension come alive, always. It is not automatic. Without our collaboration, intelligence, and freedom, even our spirit is as if struck dumb more and more, is as if increasingly fossilized, becoming like material deteriorating in every moment that passes, becoming more and more degraded. Instead, no, our spirit is always growing more and more. You who have known Giovanni and Massimo better than I have to admit that theirs is a life that is growing and that, out of millions of adults, there are few "adults" like them. I do not know if we can make these affirmations, but out of a million adults there will only be two or three who are capable of "thinking," of being so aware of their growing life. Therefore, we must beg for the awareness of God, we must pray for memory, like someone mentioned before, and like Christ reminded us, that it is a memory of what has happened to us, of what happens to us, a memory of our destiny. We should beg to be aware, that is, to be men. Otherwise, we are prey to what happens, dragged along by what happens. On the contrary, if you are on the brow of a hill and down below there is a river that flows in a certain way and you see, at a certain point, from afar, a small boat that goes against the current, you say, "There is a man over there." This is man in the world, this is man on the earth, this is man in the life of everything. Everything moves toward its degradation and its end, but man presses on. Certainly, we need energy; we should ask for the energy of awareness and of freedom. But, let's say this, may heaven will it, that, thanks to the intercession of Giovanni and Massimo, you may truly learn the School of Community of this year: the heart. We need the heart to be able to go against the current; then, when we see all the men around us, near and far, and everything they know how to express, work together with such a sad, such a desperate foolishness, so full of lies, work together in the decay of everything, how important it is—I reflect again—that we have a tight-knit companionship. Then we will live this companionship much more, we will understand much more, we will experience the continuity of the presence of Giovanni and Massimo. It is one of the most vivid memories of my life when my poor father died many years ago, my poor father, because, following the funeral car, I understood with great clarity that he was more present than before—he understood me, he loved me, and daily life did not make this experience diminish one bit.

Speaker: Excuse me if I ask you a personal question, but, at the last School of Community, Tonino said to me, "We need to begin to ask for a judgment on the things we don't normally ask." And I would like to ask this: this history for me is no longer something to speak about like some fact I encountered, but represents the dimension toward which my heart and my mind stretch. To belong

Assembly of the Community of Communion and Liberation in Campania

means to allow this history to touch everything, really everything, because even the smallest gap, I feel, can distance me from what I know constitutes me. This gap, for me, is the affective life. I ask you how to judge it, because I think that what you will say to me will be for me a good and, believe me, I do not say this sentimentally, but with the greatest reason my mind can have because, for me, the more time passes, the more I recognize, reading Giovanni especially, the more I discover that for him there was no difference between the things to ask and the things not to ask, and I think this is also the path for me.

Giussani: How can you judge it? If we ask, even where we do not understand and even where all our resistance seems to stubbornly hold on, if we ask that the fullness of life may happen, that what we belong to may happen. The Bible, we recalled at the Exercises, is the religious history of humanity and ends with two words: "Come, Lord" (*Revelation* 22:20). Because everything belongs to the mystery of God, everything, and therefore everything exists because this Mystery is present in everything, and it is this belonging to God that makes all things hold together in unity. And in fact, we have not lost, but we have acquired a relationship with Giovanni and Massimo that we would never have imagined, and if our awareness will become increasingly more mature, the much more and much sooner this will become experience. Therefore ask, ask Christ, ask His Spirit, ask Giovanni and Massimo, that in truth everything may become a help on the path, in the test. Ask the Lord also to come in your affective relationships; this is not the moment to explain to you what will happen—it will become truer, it will become true. I do not know any other phenomenon, and you know this well, for which man breaks through his limits, the limit in which he is a prisoner, in which he is buried, "entombed." There is nothing that opens "the closed limits of our hiding place," as Tarkovsky said, if not this asking. It is asking that breaks open the limit. Outside of asking—what weakness, what tiredness, what confusion! And it is grace, meaning the goodness and love of the One to whom we belong, that can answer it.

"The problem is to find something on which we can fix our attention in order to overcome our difficulties. [What is the essential element on which to place our attention for the overcoming of the difficulties, for example, the narrowness of affections? It is the ultimate reason for which that thing exists. If you put the accent on the ultimate reason for which that thing exists, then you overcome the difficulty that the path implies.] I need to focus on these areas: study, perfectionism, introversion, pensiveness, scrupulosity, vigilance, gossip. For each of these things, I need to pay particular attention. Understand, though, that if my mind is fixed on some area, it is not focused on others. Is there a center on which I can place my attention, concentrate my energy, to avoid being dispersed in a multitude of areas, and which, at the same time, allows me to walk a path that encompasses everything, without leaving anything out [this is the supreme duty of reason, this is what the heart demands]? I need, at this point, to expand upon that Christian hypothesis: 'Seek first the Kingdom and His righteousness and all these things will be given to you besides' (*Matthew* 6:33)." That for which everything is made—if I keep it in mind in a thing that I am doing—if I keep the whole in mind in what I am doing, the thing that I am doing becomes great, which means it becomes "more." "Whoever follows me will have eternal life and the hundredfold here below" (*Matthew* 19:28–29), such that even death becomes life. When the current rector of the State University of Milan lost two children in a car crash due to the fog on the highway between Bergamo and Milan, coming back from a ski trip, when his children were burned up in the car, at the end of the funeral he greeted me and said—it was a little after Christmas, January 8—"But is it true or not that I have the feeling that this is the real Christmas?" I do not remember the exact words, but the concept was this. And I told him, "Professor, this is the concept of the first Christians for which the *dies natalis* [day of birth] was the day of death. There is no stronger hypothesis, nothing that transforms, that reads reality like this." A week later the father of one of his students died, and he came to a parish on the outskirts of Milan, where there was still serious fog every night and, in the end, while he was leaving that little church, he said, "Is it possible that one should come to these gestures to be able to feel, even from afar, what joy is?" And that is the word that Emmanuel Mounier repeated to his wife in his letters, when their little girl was totally disabled. "We need, at this point, to develop that Christian hypothesis: 'Seek first the Kingdom and.. all these rest will be given to you besides.'" Saint Paul—how many times have we remembered it—says it this way: "Whether you eat or whether you drink, whether you are awake or asleep, whether you live or die, remember: you belong to Christ" (1 *Corinthians* 10:31). It is the same belonging that Giovanni mentions elsewhere. This is why we get up in the morning, for something great that embraces everything; and it is only for this reason that our actions are not asymptotic, not juxtaposed to each other like little grains of dust blown by the wind: they can touch each other tangentially, bump into each other, but they are not united, this is the comparison that the Bible says in the first *Psalm* of David: "He is like a tree planted near streams of water, that yields its fruit in season; its leaves never wither; whatever he does prospers. But not so are the wicked, not so! They are like chaff driven by the wind" (*Psalm* 1:4). All our actions are chaff, our days are like dust, if there is not this unifying center. But it is a matter of seeking, and insofar as one is small or does not have the stature of this man, of this, our great companion, then we understand that time passes. But with the passing of time, we understand more and more, and very quickly this understanding becomes a total embrace; one really begins in this world to lose nothing.

Speaker: I notice the presence of my brother now stronger and truer with respect to before, in the sense that now I can no longer cheat in comparing myself, even if in the relationship with him there was always a deep sincerity, but that minimum of fear "to put myself out" is no longer there. I no longer have that fear. I wanted to know about this presence and this companionship of Giovanni that I feel every day. In what way can it help me and what relation is there with that presence of the Mystery about which you speak?

Giussani: It is the same, because he lives in this Mystery, he subsists in it. It is a word that Saint Paul said, that he reminded the philosophers of Athens, in the Areopagus: "In this mystery we live and move and have our being" (cf. *Acts* 17:28). For Giovanni, this is already, already, without parallel, totally true, therefore it is the same identical thing. And I wish for you, Pina—in the way and the time that the Spirit will fix—that this may become also the habitual way that you see people and things in your life. Giovanni says it elsewhere, remembering in a powerful way the idea of sign that is in *The Religious Sense*. What does it mean that something is a sign? In its truth, reality is a sign, that is, a calling to something else that is within it and is more than it. Like the life that we do not give ourselves in this moment, there is within us the spring of life that is more than us. So that now, for now, the thought of Giovanni and the question of Giovanni are identified with the thought and the question of the Mystery, and tomorrow the relationship with your parents, with your friends, with the people that you will see walking in the street, with sadness thinking about all that they don't think about, with sadness thinking about their small humanity—like the dry ground on which, with difficulty, a blade of grass is born... In all these relationships, you will see that ultimate perspective of things that is the "Mystery," or that Presence in the presence of things that is the Mystery. Because nothing is made of itself. Thinking about these things with intensity, it sometimes feels like our backs are overburdened, as if they were crushed, and instead you need to resist this impression, because the result is a life a hundred times more intense.

We must ask to "re-dimension" our lives.

Speaker: What this event provoked in me, and then the Spiritual Exercises, is the re-centering of the question, that is, the search for companionship in life, the search for what makes life precious. I had almost lost this question in the period immediately preceding these facts. While remaining in the companionship, I no longer sought it;. These facts, that is, the death of Giovanni and Massimo and the Exercises, have brought these things out into the open—I was in the Movement without asking about its meaning for my life. Now I want to know how much the recognition that this is the most important thing depends on my will, while not thinking that it depends simply on me.

Giussani: It depends on your will, because you can ask, "God, if you are there, reveal yourself to me." This prayer of the atheist, of the Unnamed from Manzoni, is the minimum of the human level, of the human capacity, the minimum. Less than this and man is no longer man; therefore, it depends on us at least to ask the question, at least to beg. Like for an adult man that has a responsibility, the greatest sin would be habitual forgetfulness, which is an irresponsibility, and so the responsibility that we have in our life is not to forget the goal, and this not-forgetting is not something abstract. It translates into asking and searching, but this is already something more complicated.

Before finishing, I want to re-read together—did you all get these pages? —"Our pain [we understand already the nobility of the soul; for a noble soul, for a soul that is not small-minded; the pain is to see people being stingy; finiteness is a pain for a great soul, not for a small one] stems from the fact that we have come to live outside of the horizon of the sacred [of the sacred, of the religious sense, that is, of the ultimate sense, of the Ultimate for which we got up this morning, for which we came here from far away today, for which we are gathered here, for which we will rest tonight]. Our everyday horizon changes with the changing circumstances. [Terrible! It is like the dust in the wind.] But the horizon that is defined by the circumstances is suffocating; attractive at the beginning, it then becomes boring. Living within this type of horizon, we adjust and try to put the pieces of ourselves in order [it is Tarkovsky's notion of the hiding place]. But the numbers never add up. By horizon, we mean that which immediately comes to your mind.... Even though we can sometimes fool ourselves into believing that we need something now that is [in itself] objectively illusory, still, we cannot fool ourselves about our desire for life, a desire that is disturbed by the thought of death. Here it becomes clear that only God can resolve this problem." But if only God is the solution of life, only God is the solution of your affective relationship, and only God is the solution of your efforts in both study and work, only God is the solution. Solution, that is, the exact perspective, the right pace of your walking, of your driving in the car, of your return to your house, of the patience with which you have to put up with a person who bothers you, of the ability to forgive everything, everything. Therefore, Saint Paul gave to the most ignorant, to the poorest Christians of that time, the most beautiful definition of criticism, that is, the capacity to use reason: "Test everything, retain what is good" (1 *Thessalonians* 5:21). Retain what is good, what "has value." But what is the thing that "has value"? What is a value? It is the relationship between the horizon that we have immediately in front of us and destiny. And it is this relationship that is the measure of what we do; even the littlest gesture of the housewife who puts the kitchen in order is great, can be great. Great, because the measure of an action is the heart.

And so Giovanni teaches us. Humanly speaking, when—I beg you to tell me, friends—when have you heard people talk like this? Certainly, he spoke like this, but when did you understand that he spoke like this? Now, in his words, there is a power—still enigmatic to us—of his continuous, eternal, inexorable presence. Like Pina said, now we can no longer cheat, and in fact we will try not to think about it—this supreme cowardice that we will help each other avoid at all costs. Deep down, why does a man marry a woman, if not to be helped to walk? For this reason, friendship is the source of the measure of everything. This is the place where the measure of everything is recalled, and this is the place where Giovanni and Massimo remain without the possibility of darkness.

Funeral Homily

Father Giacomo Tantardini

February 22, 1988
Parish of Saint Gennaro
Benevento, Italy

Earlier, at Giovanni's house, a friend showed me a phrase that Giovanni had written just a few days ago and that now I would like to read to you as a help to live this great pain, to live it with that dignity and with that peace and with that humble gratitude that faith in Jesus Christ gives to man, makes possible for man. So, he wrote a few days ago, meditating, reading a lesson from Father Giussani: "Even though we can sometimes fool ourselves into believing that we need something now that is objectively illusory, still, we cannot fool ourselves about our desire for life, a desire that is disturbed by the thought of death. Here it becomes clear that only God can resolve this problem."

If we can fool ourselves like all of us fool ourselves—and we do fool ourselves, and maybe we spend hours and days, weeks and months and years in this deceit—if we can fool ourselves into believing that we need something that is illusory, yet if one listens to the voice of the heart, that voice of which we sang at the beginning: "Poor is the voice of a man that does not exist, such is our voice if it no longer has a reason...," if one listens to the voice of his heart, he realizes that the heart desires something greater. He realizes that the heart desires something that all the things of this world cannot give. He realizes that there is a desire for life and this desire for life is disturbed by death. Because even death is a part of man's life, of the life of every man, of the life of each of us, and it is when death touches us personally, when it touches us because it touches people we love so much, and then in front of that heart, of this *desire for life disturbed by death*, of this desire for life wounded by death, then everything is clear, then it is clear that only God is the answer. And you see, every person has this clarity, the heart of man, when it is true, when it does not suffocate this desire, this voice, has this clarity. In some instances, for example when a pain that is so great passes through our life, this clarity is everything, is clear: only God, only the Mystery can be the answer to this desire. With all our *giving ourselves something to do* and with all our *agitation* or with all our not thinking about these things, yet this voice remains. And then only something other can respond. You see this clarity, which is the clarity that Jesus had when He met someone who was wounded by a pain that was so great, when he meets that mother who was carrying her son to the cemetery and he tells her, "Don't cry." Yes, this clarity belongs to every man. When in front of pain one says, "Don't cry," this clarity is evident. But Giovanni saw with this clarity, saw it in an encounter; it is an encounter that makes it clear, that makes this clarity shine. It is an encounter that reveals to man that only God is the answer to his heart and reveals it to him because He offers him the answer, because He offers it and communicates it to him like the Gospel of Zacchaeus that we read. When Jesus looked up and said, "Zacchaeus I am coming to your house," that instant, that gaze, that word communicated to that man everything that his heart was waiting for. And this is how it was for Giovanni: it was an encounter, a most-human encounter, an encounter that leaves man in his humility and in his nothingness, and yet changes everything.

An encounter makes that clarity luminous and certain; an encounter makes this clarity the most evident and realistic thing in life: that only God is the answer, not like an article of belief, not like the clarity of a moment, but like a luminous nearness, like a friendship, like when a mother holds a baby and the baby falls asleep, like a real and powerful friendship. How great is the Grace of encountering here, in this life, even before seeing Him face to face, encountering the Answer to our heart! How great is this Grace of being able to walk, here, in this life, with this ability to be close to Him! And this answer, and this nearness is infinitely greater than the awareness that one has of it, greater than the shyness with which one manages to speak about this communion.

So I wanted to say to his family and to the people that loved Giovanni the most that now this closeness and this friendship is possible, now it can be greater, because you see that nearness does not by itself bring communion, does not by itself make you friends. Instead, there is with Giovanni now a nearness that is so luminous, so clear, so real that nothing can damage it. This closeness now is greater. The encounter that we have had makes this nearness indestructible, makes this nearness an experience. One has the experience that people who have had the same encounter, people who have been friends, even when one of them dies, even when the nearness is no longer visible, but even after death, this nearness, instead of diminishing, becomes greater. This nearness becomes greater because one is aware and is aware in *real* life, and it is a nearness which can say *you*, like when you see each other, a nearness that can ask for help; like when you see each other, this nearness becomes greater, this friendship becomes greater. And you see, even in my experience, there is a Fact that gives me certainty that this nearness is greater and is like an overabundance of Grace. When the Lord passes through our life with suffering, and with a suffering as great as the suffering of death, it is because He promises us a superabundant Grace. Because it is really true that our friends who are in Paradise do miracles, it is really true that our friends who are in Paradise multiply the Grace among us, and it is through this Grace that we grow, that one is certain that death no longer divides, that death does not separate us anymore. One is certain that the encounter—through which the answer to the heart was communicated—is more powerful even than death. And it is because we have this certainty, because our life, our intelligence, and our freedom have this certainty, that we can, even in this moment, give thanks to the Lord.

www.ingramcontent.com/pod-product-compliance
Lightning Source LLC
Chambersburg PA
CBHW020200090426
42734CB00008B/889